9000951146

Quantum speed reading works: I have seen it in action. It is further evidence that when the brain is not under the domination of the left hemisphere—as in children, and in adults in altered states of consciousness—it can operate in the "quantum processing mode" where vast amounts of information can be accessed almost instantly. Speed reading is among the phenomena that we need to look at seriously, in order to improve our habitual capacity to pick up, and also to send, information entire dimensions beyond the power of the classical operating mode of the left hemisphere.

—Ervin Laszlo, author,
Science and the Akashic Field

QUANTUM SPEED READING

Awakening Your Child's Mind

Yumiko Tobitani

HAMPTON ROADS
PUBLISHING COMPANY, INC.

for the evolving human spirit

Translated from the Japanese by Echan Deravy
Edited for English edition by John Nelson

Cover design by Steve Amarillo
Cover digital image of the book © Getty Images, Inc.
All other cover images © Jupiterimages Corp. All rights reserved.

Hampton Roads Publishing Company, Inc.
1125 Stoney Ridge Road
Charlottesville, VA 22902

434-296-2772
fax: 434-296-5096
e-mail: hrpc@hrpub.com
www.hrpub.com

If you are unable to order this book from your local
bookseller, you may order directly from the publisher.
Call 1-800-766-8009, toll-free.

Library of Congress Cataloging-in-Publication Data

Tobitani, Yumiko, 1944-
  [Jissen hado sokudokuho. English]
  Quantum speed-reading : awakening your child's mind / Yumiko Tobitani ;
translated from the Japanese by Echan Deravy.
      p. cm.
  Summary: "A Japanese teacher describes the discovery of a new technique that taps
directly into the power of the right brain, allowing us to unlock our intuitive nature
to promote education, help improve memory, boost concentration, and more.
Includes a program for toddlers as well as exercises for both children and adults"--
Provided by publisher.
  ISBN 1-57174-471-1 (5 1/2 x 8 1/2 tp : alk. paper)
  1. Speed reading. 2. Cerebral dominance. 3. Brain--Localization of
functions. 4. Left and right (Psychology) 5. Imagery (Psychology) 6.
Visualization. I. Title.
  LB1050.54.T63 2006
  428.4'3--dc22
                              2005033860

ISBN 1-57174-471-1
10 9 8 7 6 5 4 3 2 1
Printed on acid-free paper in Canada

Contents

1: The Emergence of Quantum Speed-Reading   1

If My Students Can Do It, Everyone Can! • Even a Foreign Language Book Can Be Read Easily • Learning to Use the Function of Automatic Processing • The Student Who Wrote a Letter to Professor Hawking • Perceiving Sounds and Smells Coming from Books • Easily Memorizing Textbooks, Too • How Colors Show Levels of Comprehension • Seeing Trains from the Time Schedule! • A New Concept Emerges • Feelings of Oneness Are Engendered • Quantum Speed-Reading Makes Poets of the Children

2: Quantum Speed-Reading Helps with Exams   14

Sudden Improvement in Grades through the Energy of Cooperation • Passing the Azabu Middle School Exam with a Completely New Way of Learning • The Three Pillars of Right-Brain Learning • Freely Using All Three Parts of the Brain to Live Naturally • Having Fun Studying Is the Key to Learning

Foreword

A Message from Makoto Shichida, Head of the Shichida Child Academy

Ms. Yumiko Tobitani, a top teacher at the Shichida child academy, has written this book about the theory and practice of Quantum Speed-Reading. Quantum Speed-Reading is a unique form of speed-reading that utilizes the right brain to visualize the contents of a book and instantly grasp its meaning. Conventional speed-reading utilizes the left brain to quickly read and understand printed text. The right brain doesn't read text word for word but rather grasps the general content at the level of thought vibration (the quantum level) and then converts those impressions into images or words to be read. This is a basic function of the right brain with its "sympathetic resonance" ability to translate written words into correlated images.

The basis of quantum speed-reading consists first and foremost in opening the right brain's imaging capability. This cannot be done without first fostering your clear imaging powers. As you read this book, you will find many amazing examples of children using the right brain to access information "vibrationally" and then translate that into images. The right brain's imaging ability has the power to memorize text via images, to heal sickness using images, and to express these images perfectly in stories.

The educational application of right-brain imaging power has never before been utilized in this manner. The Shichida Child Academy has pioneered this previously unknown technique for unleashing the brain's imaging power. Quantum Speed-Reading is the ultimate technique for using the power of our brain's cerebrum. This book is based on case studies of how Quantum Speed-Reading evolved into an actual methodology. It is my fervent wish that this technique be of service to as many people as possible.

Prologue

Quantum Speed-Reading (QSR) awakens the diencephalon area (the area that connects the brain hemispheres) of the midbrain. The key to that awakening lies in the natural imaging ability of children. In using QSR in our classrooms, our students have seen a variety of abilities blossom. Simply by flipping the pages of a book, many have been able to understand its content; others have seen the future and have even at times been able to sense different types of energy via telepathy. Although some adults discount these claims, most of our students have simply accepted these types of abilities at face value. Perhaps it is their natural acceptance that allows such abilities to blossom. The following essay is by one of our young students, T. G. (from the Kasai School):

My Encounter with Shichida Training

If I were asked what has been the best thing about Shichida training, I would right away answer, "I have learned how to create images and do many things with them." Image training is used in all our Shichida schools and has become second nature to me, and lately I have been feeling that this is something really wonderful. Imaging can be used in many situations, plus it is really simple to use. For example, remembering textbook material or study notes is a "left-brained" exercise. But using the right brain to memorize is fun and is so smoothly done. In the past, I used to hate this convenient imaging ability. I've been doing this image training at the Shichida School since I was a little kid. I couldn't get why we were supposed to imagine a red ball all the time and thought it was meaningless because I didn't know how to use it. As I carried on with the training, such feelings led to stress and a strong dislike for those images in me. Despite getting the Shichida training at such a young age, there were no visible results when I was little. But this began to change when I entered elementary school. A painting I had done of a crayfish based on an image was selected for study. [Please see color section.] I still remember this clearly. By moving that crayfish around inside my head, changing its color, or changing my angle of looking at it, I woke up to the fun of being able to change the image freely. At first, I was shocked, but later on I got the feeling that these images are great. It was after that I was able to do lots of things with imagery. These are some of them.

Treating Sickness

Whenever someone in my family gets sick, I get called right away. I see that there is a virus in the painful areas or the feverish parts of the sick person. So then I visualize becoming a micro person and going inside their bodies to heal them. Then they start to get better, so we don't use drugs in our house.

School Study

When I need to memorize something, I make up a story and remember it with images. For example, if I have to remember something about history, I imagine I am a historical person of that era, and no matter how difficult the theme is I get it easily.

Getting Motivated

When I decide to do something but I don't have much enthusiasm, I imagine in detail that I have already succeeded in achieving it. When I do that, it is not just a picture (in my head) but also has the sounds, sensations, and feelings that I imagine. Things go 100 percent well when I vividly imagine other people around me who are happy about it.

So I have done lots of things with image training, but what outdoes everything else easily and has the greatest potential is the Quantum Speed-Reading. I found out about this from Ms. Tobitani at the Kasai school and started doing it. From the moment I started, I "got" this ability even though it is difficult to learn. Since I had previously done the image training that it is based on, all I had to do was shift my thinking. There is no way to compare how much faster I have gotten at reading textbooks and study notes through doing QSR. After about a year, I took the entrance exams for middle school. When things were not going well with the study, I imagined myself doing well and was able to get over the problem. Then when it came to deciding on which was the best school to choose, I suddenly had an image of Azabu Middle School and my future school life there.

When I asked my prep school teacher for advice, however, he said, "It's dangerous for you to change your school of choice now. And especially getting into Azabu Middle School, which is known to be difficult. You should shoot for a school that you know for sure you'll get into!" When I heard that, I swore I would get into Azabu! So right away, I went to the front gate of Azabu Middle School and had my picture taken standing there. Then I looked at the photo every day. After that, my prep school grades started getting better and better. Then, on the entrance-exam day, I imagined myself studying at that school. At that moment, all the tension went away and I was able to relax and take the exam. For the difficult questions, I just closed my eyes and saw the textbook I had speed-read "vibrationally" and got the answer from it. I saw how amazing the image training is because the test results came out just as I had visualized. Thanks to image training and Quantum Speed-Reading, I entered my school of choice, Azabu Middle School.

I feel good about having done the Shichida training all this time. At the Shichida schools, they tend to think that everything happens at the preschool level with the training, but in my case it started in elementary school, so nobody should give up but should carry on with it. I am most grateful to Ms. Tobitani of the Kasai school and to both my parents. When I become a parent, I want to teach my children the Shichida method. I will be actualizing my visualization of reading this essay in front of everyone in November.

In 2002, on the fifteenth anniversary of the Shichida Child Academy, we called for essays to be written and collected from all over Japan on the theme "My encounter with Shichida training." The essay you have just read was selected as the best and, in that same year in November at the memorial event, T. G. actually did stand up in front of everyone and read it!

1

The Emergence of Quantum Speed-Reading

After flipping through a book in English, a second-grader said
[in Japanese], "Hey, this is interesting!"
Right away, I asked, "How come?"
"Well, it's about a swordfish," he replied.
The book was Hemingway's The Old Man and the Sea.

If My Students Can Do It, Everyone Can!

Children have a great variety of natural abilities. One of them is called Quantum Speed-Reading. Unlike the normal way of reading one line at a time, QSR involves quickly flipping through a book and picking up the thought vibrations emanating from it, and then translating those vibrations into light or imagery-based information through which the content is instantly understood.

One day I had my class first quickly, then slowly, flip through the pages of a book for a total of 30 times. The children moved their own chairs to a spot where they felt most relaxed and proceeded to flip through the pages of the book. After finishing, they came back to their desks. One child, however, was totally absorbed and continued long after the others had returned. I thought, "Oh well, I'll just leave him," and I went on to the next lesson. Then I heard the sound of a chair being dragged back across the floor, and there was the child back at his desk. Then he said, "That was really fun." When students show any change in their speech or behavior, I generally try to listen to them. So I asked the child, "What's up, then?"

"I mean the pictures came out of the book and I understood everything" was the reply I got from this second-year elementary school child! On a daily basis, I always try to theorize about the phenomena that the children display, in other words, the abilities they demonstrate. In this case, I realized immediately that this was a function of the right brain's imagery at work with this child. Since the right brain processes information with great speed, I gathered that when a book is flipped through at high speed, the words are transformed into images and come out as pictures.

Naturally, my students were baffled and sat there amazed. I decided to have some of my other students have a try at it. We repeated the previous exercise, but this time with an expectation that something would happen. All of them did exactly the same thing, flipping through the pages, and, amazingly, they all saw images in their minds.

The right brain has the ability to communicate information so that it is understandable to everyone. This is called *resonance*. Therefore, when we have a desire to learn something or the desire to see it, this ability transmits it to us at a vibrational (quantum) level. This was an entirely new way of reading books, and I decided to call it Quantum Speed-Reading.

Even a Foreign Language Book Can Be Read Easily

If when my student had not returned to his desk with the others, I had scolded him, saying, "What's wrong with you, everybody's being held up!" I believe that Quantum Speed-Reading would never have emerged as a practice. I don't believe children should be left entirely to do as they please. The ability central to QSR, however, is one that comes naturally from children being spontaneous. If I had scolded the boy, this ability might not have been discovered.

From that moment on, all kinds of abilities started to blossom and, for some time afterward, I was completely wrapped up in having the children flip the pages of books. The children didn't think of this as school study. They were doing it as play, as a game. But even so, there came a time when they started to lose interest. So in order to change their focus, I handed out English books for these Japanese children to speed-read. These were not picture books but books full of text in English. The children, who could not read English, flipped through them about ten times and said nothing. I thought to myself that this was not going to turn out well. But before long, a second-grader said, "Hey, this is interesting!"

Right away, I asked, "How come?"

"Well, it's about a swordfish," he replied.

The book was Hemingway's *Old Man and the Sea*. The boy then went on to tell me about the story. Thinking that perhaps he had read the book in Japanese or been told the story, I asked him, "Do you know the book *The Old Man and the Sea*?"

"What's that?" was the reply.

He knew absolutely nothing about the work in question and, since he could not read English, it was very strange that he had been able to understand the content.

So I asked, "How were you able to read it?"

He replied, "Even though the book is written in English, when I do the Quantum Speed-Reading, hiragana, katakana, and kanji (Japanese scripts) come out on the right page, and in the middle there is an image so I get all of it."

Learning to Use the Function of Automatic Processing

In the right brain, there is a function called *automatic processing*. Perhaps this ability allows the mind to translate automatically any language when the reading speed is increased. There also exists the function of imaging anything and of transforming any written words into pictures. The operation of these two functions combined with the fact that many children spontaneously embrace them has resulted in all of our students being able to create this phenomenon. They can Quantum Speed-Read books in languages they don't know: English, French, or German; it makes no difference. This can be thought of, then, as the universal translation function of the brain's internal computer.

The Student Who Wrote a Letter to Professor Hawking

An interesting thing happened when we did Quantum Speed-Reading on Stephen Hawking's book *The Universe in a Nutshell* published in Japanese by Kadokawa Shoten Publishing.

S. K., a second-grader, said, "Professor Hawking has overlooked something, so I have to tell him about it."

I was a little taken aback, thinking that we would have to send the message in English. At this point, S. K. said he would speak in English. He sat in front of the video recorder and started off by introducing himself, then said there were many kinds of black holes and, although other people could not see them, he himself could use imagery to peer deep into space. He spoke all this in fluent English. Later, S. K.'s insight was verified by a newspaper report stating that there are indeed many kinds of black holes. The book in question is pretty difficult reading even for adults. Young K said, "If Professor Hawking could change his way of looking at the black holes from being based on looking from here, to looking from *there*, he would gain a slightly different perspective on the matter." I was really amazed.

Young K. is now awaiting a reply from professor Hawking to the following letter:

"How I felt after QS reading **The Universe in a Nutshell**
by Stephen Hawking" (translated by Katsuhiko Sata),
by S. K., second-grade elementary student
of the Kasai school of Shichida training

My name is K—. I like to think about space and I like to imagine. So I think about black holes. There are many kinds of black holes. Even if you don't see them, I can see far into space using my imaging power. And I can see right now a black hole. You may think it exists or it does not exist, but I can really see the blue-colored black hole. I think the blue black hole can suck up and eat other black holes. I hate to think about the time when the two black holes come together because they do make a big black hole.

But I do like this one thing about the black holes. When it's born, the black hole has a pole in the middle. And I like the color of the pole. It's like white purple for me. And I like the stars going round the black hole, because the black hole can suck in anything. The stars will go together like a ring, a beautiful ring. And I like the ring; I wish they were diamond stars, so it would be a colorful ring. I hate to think of the black hole when it comes to the Earth. Do you hate it? I know this because I see good images. It's like having an antenna on my head.

Perceiving Sounds and Smells Coming from Books

In our daily lives, we adults live with a left-brain focus on language. Or to put it another way, we hardly ever use the imagery of the right brain. In Shichida training, we place great emphasis on further activating the right brain. To understand this technique, adults must first step outside the "box" of left-brain thinking. Children, on the other hand, naturally use right-brain imagery to activate many abilities.

With the children, we did Quantum Speed-Reading of a foreign language library collection as a kind of game. We then noticed a child flipping the pages with his ear held next to the book. When considered from a left-brain point of view, this would seem nonsensical. When I asked the child what he was doing, he replied, "This way I can begin to hear sounds."

By flipping the book next to one's ear, sounds that should not be sensed are heard with the QSR technique. To give a concrete example, one student told of hearing the bang of a rifle shot at a bear and the splashing sound of the bear falling into the sea. By holding books next to their noses and flipping the pages, other children were able to sense smells, such as rice burning, a pickled plum, or dried fish. In stories in which a person fell into the sea, the children said, in voices that sounded like they had stuffed noses, "It's so cold!" It thus seemed that they were having an experience of being in real time in the place described in the book.

It appears that by stimulating the right brain and its nonphysical-based sense organs, a general mobilization occurs in their functioning. In other words, the right brain is sensing things without using physical organs of perception as the left brain does.

Easily Memorizing Textbooks, Too

When we considered how to use this ability, we inevitably ended up with the idea of applying it in schools as a learning tool. With that in mind, we had the children flip the pages of textbooks and they were amazed by the results. Flipping through arithmetic textbooks actually resulted in the answers jumping out. Furthermore, it wasn't just the answers that appeared; they came along with their equations, since the test questions required the method used to solve them. Once again, the automatic processing function inside the brain's computer was at work. I think this function perceives the overall context and, in this case, figured that a math question in sentence form required an equation as part of the answer.

We next tried flipping through textbooks dealing with Japanese language studies. We found that in poetry sections images of flying butterflies would appear, along with a great variety of other images.

After a while, I began to think that perhaps these children were memorizing text in the process of flipping through the pages. When I asked if they were memorizing, they said they didn't know if they were or not. When we tested it, we found that memorization of the entire book was occurring. And it wasn't just one child who could do this, but every single one. I was shocked. How was it that simply by flipping through the pages of a book, they could memorize it and repeat all of its contents?

How Colors Show Levels of Comprehension

As we continued with these kinds of lessons, colors began to appear to the students as they flipped the pages. In the years of doing this, a great deal of data has accumulated. For example, at times, the seven rainbow colors appear or striped patterns or just single colors. It seems that poor comprehension ability is related to the colors red, yellow, and orange. When green, blue, purple, and indigo appear, the level of comprehension is higher; thus the content is better understood. When red appears, the children don't understand the content because they have never learned about it. White indicates that they understand the content instinctively, whether they have learned it previously or not.

It was in this way that I began to see that there is a profound relationship between the depth of understanding and the colors that appear. Both green and blue signal understanding, though the latter denotes a higher comprehension. Orange signals no understanding. The reds indicate no understanding because the content hasn't been previously studied, whereas yellow means it's hard to understand.

The colors appear to fan out in the space above the pages that are being flipped. It's not the cover or the picture inside the book that's being reflected at all. And if you want to change the colors, you can. There are times when stripes appear, or when red and blue both appear at the same time. At such times, the children are "reading" the content, but they do not really understand it.

The Color Coming from the Book Indicates Comprehension

Color	Level of Comprehension
White	Able to understand without having studied material
Purple	Can understand
Indigo	Can understand
Blue	Can understand
Green	Can understand
Yellow	Cannot understand (partially)
Orange	Cannot understand
Red	Cannot understand because have not studied material

Seeing Trains from the Time Schedule!

The next exercise we tried was to read more technical material. We used a train schedule. Because it had a photograph on its cover, we blindfolded the children or covered the cover with something so they couldn't see it. Then they flipped through the pages. Afterward they said things like, "I can see the bullet train," "I can see railroad tracks," "I can see a station," "I can see a landscape," or "I can see lots of numbers in rows." When it comes to train schedules, it is not about understanding the content, that is, the departure and arrival times. In this case, the columns of numbers are immediately transformed into destinations or rail routes.

Next, we had the idea of flipping through planning drafts to see if anything would pop out when in fact nothing physical existed at the "location." We used the test paper for the architects' exam, from the second-class exam category. We thought this would be interesting since there was nothing but draft drawings on it. We went ahead and the children saw completed wooden houses. It was only later that we found out that second-class architects are not allowed to use concrete in house construction, but only wood. In this case, the imagery emerged with precise accuracy down to the finest details.

To top that exercise, we next chose musical scores to flip through, and the children heard the music playing! We tried high-school differential calculus and physics textbooks, too. The children reported seeing red coming from inside parts of the book. In other words, they could not understand those parts because they had not yet learned that material. In the part about the four rules of arithmetic, they picked up blue because they had previously learned these calculation methods. Such exercises are how we discovered that reds and blues are related to levels of comprehension.

A New Concept Emerges

One day an editor came to our class to report on our progress. Although he had a basic understanding of Quantum Speed-Reading, his eyes grew larger on seeing children in a classroom matter-of-factly doing speed-reading exercises with results that would normally be considered miraculous.

He asked us how all this was possible. I replied that it is conceivable that the brain has a function that can automatically take letter-based language information and transform it into images. I explained further how levels of comprehension can be measured via the change in the colors experienced. I told him that if this were all there was to it, it would simply be a phenomenon. But I wondered whether this approach could be utilized as a way of learning through the right brain, and whether changing the colors of the images that represent the degree of understanding could change the level of comprehension.

We next experimented with this concept. As the pages of the textbook were being flipped and colors representing low levels of comprehension such as red, orange, and yellow appeared, the children closed their eyes and used imagery to change the colors to green, blue, and purple (which represent high degrees of comprehension). When they opened their eyes, the colors had actually changed to green, blue, and purple. They now found that they could understand previously incomprehensible material. When the right brain is activated through the use of speed in this manner, I believe its translation function allows the children to comprehend such material. After all is said and done, speed is of the ultimate importance. By elevating the speed, this sort of ability and brain functioning can be achieved.

Feelings of Oneness Are Engendered

During lessons, we have the children sit around a pile of books placed in the middle of the floor. As they go about the QSR learning process, the children treat each other with consideration and affection. It is not too much to say that their individual energies become one. When they put away the books after the lesson, they take great care in arranging them in the basket where they are kept. They have come to think of the books as having an important *existence,* just as they do. This might be more than the right-brain involvement; it might be stimulation of the diencephalon itself. I think that the essence of our being human is transmitted from just such a fundamental area of the brain.

This might account for understanding not only the content of the book but also the message the author intended, as well as the feelings he or she had at the time of writing. To acquire the same information through left-brain study would involve a huge amount of effort, but these children very simply Quantum Speed-Read the essence of it all.

Quantum Speed-Reading Makes Poets of the Children

At times, children who have learned Quantum Speed-Reading write at a higher level than they are thought capable. A first-grader offhandedly wrote the following on a piece of notepaper:

Who knows, maybe we are also transmitting mind

energy. And then maybe people's minds are getting tele-pathic. If that happens, then the Earth will become beauti-ful, won't it? Then the Earth and the cosmos will get linked and won't that be good for Nature? And then maybe every-one will get on really well together. We'll be able to do some-thing for Life. Yes, definitely!

Children who learn QSR also create emotionally rich fairy tales. A third-grade student penned the following:

I, the Cherry Tree

In this long line of cherry trees, I am the only one not blossoming. That huge building over there has blocked out the sun, and so I am the only one that doesn't get the light. Little me, I don't blossom. Nobody notices me, not the other trees, not the people.

Then one day, little Akura, who always comes along this street, said, "Hey, I'm always coming along this street and this cherry tree is always feeling down." Little Akura was three years old. . . .

I had the feeling it was her always telling me I was feel-ing down.

The next day, she said, "Cherry tree, you look down again today. Is there something bothering you? Or is some-body being nasty to you? Is there something else going on?"

I replied, "That's enough, you little Akura!" Little Akura was worrying about me.

And then the next day came. I said to little Akura, "Hey, little Akura, what should I do to get accepted?"

Little Akura seemed to hear my words. "Hmmm, what should we do to get you to be accepted as a cherry tree? I know! What if you are brave whatever happens! What's important is to do something, not just know it. Even if you can't do it completely, try doing it one percent!"

Little Akura had taught me something important: Even

if you can't do it all, just try one percent. . . . "Thanks, little Akura. Thanks to you, Akura, I feel better."

"Yeah! That's great. Bye bye, cherry tree!" Little Akura's smiling face went on and on.

The next day, I heard the gentle sound of the wind and the falling petals of the other cherry trees. But I still hadn't blossomed. Then little Akura came by again. "Ah, it's you, cherry tree. Have you blossomed yet? Looks like you haven't, cherry tree."

"Yes, you're right, not me, not yet."

"It's OK, cherry tree. Look on the bright side," she said.

"Yes, OK," I said. Two weeks later, I still hadn't blossomed. The other cherry trees had all finished blooming and their blossoms were almost all gone. Soon it would be time for little Akura to come this way. Just as I was thinking that, all of a sudden my body felt heavy and I started to give off light. What was happening? Wow! A bud opened. One by one the buds opened properly. I wondered if little Akura would come along.

But on that day, little Akura was away on a trip and didn't show up. Two days later, little Akura came back. She'll be coming this way, coming right this way! I waited, throbbing full of excitement. But on this day little Akura didn't pay any attention to me. Just then . . . one by one the petals started falling off of my body.

"Hey, cherry tree!" shouted little Akura.

"Cherry tree?" said little Akura's mother, shaking her head.

And then an old man walking along the street said, shaking his head, "What's this? A cherry tree?" And then a whole bunch of people started to gather around me. On that day, I was so happy, so really happy.

Through doing Quantum Speed-Reading, the human heart is enriched, as this story illustrates. To be able to imagine oneself in the position of a tree and to write about it is the same as receiving a message directly from the tree. This is another aspect of QSR. One might say that the thoughts and feelings of an actual cherry tree have been picked up at the quantum level and put into words.

This chapter has shown how QSR can be used at fundamental levels, such as in testing student preparation and school education. One could quite conceivably apply QSR to children who are autistic or disabled in some way. We have thus discovered and developed an educational technique with limitless applications.

2

Quantum Speed-Reading Helps with Exams

There is a danger that studying will become a world of left-brain students who can and right-brain students who cannot study well.

If it is true that QSR connects us to a deeper part of our being, then it should be possible for us to perceive the future. At this point in our work, we began to use QSR to image the school of choice for each of our students. We asked what would be the best school for each to attend in order to serve society and prepare each to go out into the world. To use the example of T. G., mentioned in the prologue, he was in fifth grade when, after weekly training in QSR, the same school began to appear in his images. There were images of him walking in the courtyard of the school, playing football in the schoolyard, and studying in the school library. No name or location of the school accompanied the images. It turned out to be the Azabu Middle School. This is one of the three most prestigious secondary schools in Japan and entrance requires considerable academic skills. T. G., however, was considered to lack such ability. It was then that something interesting happened.

T. G.'s grades began to improve, earning him a double-digit position on the entry list, around number 18 or 20, then moving to a single digit place on the list. It was not the case that he started to study more. As the feeling of "I'm getting into Azabu!" penetrated the deep areas of his brain, I believe a change occurred in the quality of his brain functioning.

I believe when the information regarding Azabu reached T. G.'s diencephalon or resonated with it in some way, drastic changes happened. In other words, when the command saying "You are going to Azabu!" penetrated the essential core of the diencephalon, it caused an alignment with bringing that possibility into reality. It is just like an Othello game when one move suddenly turns everything upside down. As a result, more right brain–left brain coordination occurred, allowing T. G. to improve his grade average test by test and ultimately enter Azabu Middle School.

Sudden Improvement in Grades through the Energy of Cooperation

As to the question of whether anyone can accomplish what T. G. did, there does exist something akin to a condition. In order for such resonance to occur at the diencephalon in the brain stem, it seems necessary for cooperative feelings such as kindness, love, and peace to be present. This kind of ability requires a vibration of cooperation, which we all originally had, to activate the diencephalon. A connection then appears to happen and special abilities manifest for the first time. This is the most important point to bear in mind. It too often happens that academic advancement turns into a competition. That, in itself, is a totally left-brain orientation. Only feelings of love and cooperation can create a resonance that evokes this great capability.

To return to the entrance exams, the first step for T. G. was to flip through the pages of a Japanese language text, which resulted in the color orange. With arithmetic, the colors were green and blue. The physical sciences showed yellow. We carried on collecting data day after day. We noticed that though there were a lot of oranges and yellows in the beginning, at a certain point the colors began to change and his comprehension improved. They almost all turned into blues and greens.

Recently, one of our sixth-graders reported studying only an hour a day, though the school entrance exams were getting closer. At one point, his grades slipped from the top ten to the next rank below. The reason he gave was that the other students had started studying three or four hours a day. When T. G. began to study hard and his grades went up to second place, our sixth grader apparently felt that he was outmatched, lost his resonance ability, and dropped behind the others.

Passing the Azabu Middle School Exam with a Completely New Way of Learning

From the period of March to February of the next school year, I was collecting data as we prepared for the February secondary-school entrance exams using our QSR lessons. We had one 50-minute lesson per week of preparation, of which five minutes was devoted to QSR. When flipping through the pages of the material, the right brain would use its senses to grasp the study theme involved. After this was done, we used imagery training to integrate the students with the text contents.

For example, the message from a Japanese language text was "Read the sentences as if you had experienced them." First, an image from a story was used to get the answers to questions, and if that didn't work, the students would then put themselves into the story and write down the feelings that arose. After that, the students would read the sentences written down to search for the answers and underline them and thus fill in the blanks to the questions. There was even a message about paying close attention to the particularly hard questions to understand the answers better. This, of course, relates to left-brain study. Using imagery to place oneself in a certain position, however, made abundant use of the right brain's unique sensitivity. We can see that this is a left-brain way of learning with right-brain components added. With arithmetic questions, students would write their unsolved problems in their notebooks and later would get a message about how to solve the problem.

Then there were other messages such as: "If you listen to the teacher's ideas, you can get the answers"; "You can get rid of the problem of totally missing the answers"; and "You can solve problems that are similar." If the students did exactly what the messages indicated, blue colors would begin to appear.

Because the physical sciences were several levels more difficult, there were more reds appearing. At that point, we got the message, "Don't just use memory, but also use arithmetic to solve it; remember stars by using imagery and recheck your calculations."

The Shichida method has a technique to remember things through a science and sociology song. The technique is called the *Shichida Memorization Method*. The result of using this is that the colors all change to blues. This is exactly what one would expect from a right-brain technique.

The subject of sociology can be learned using this technique. Even when the students thought they had a full grasp of the information, some parts were forgotten and so the color orange emerged. Then we used the imaging memorization technique. The students used QSR on the text and solved problems that were similar in nature. At this point, yellows emerged.

Facts in geography and history can also be memorized using imagery. The process for remembering famous historical figures is interesting. First, you create an image of the historical setting, then you become that person at that time in history. For example, if you want to remember facts about Ieyasu Tokugawa (Japan's first Shogun in the 1600s), then you become Ieyasu Tokugawa. You go beyond the limits of space and of time. You venture to that historical time period to become Ieyasu Tokugawa and surround yourself with the people and scenery there, seeing it all around you. Using this memorization technique, you will remember the year and the name of the historical figure. This is a completely new way of learning.

The Three Pillars of Right-Brain Learning

As we continued studying in this way, green would appear when we were doing Japanese lessons. We solved sentence questions and remembered words and phrases in kanji characters. In arithmetic, there were many new things to be learned, so the teacher taught our students the QSR method of solving problems. At this juncture, the colors were coming up yellow and so imagery was used to change them to blue. With the physical sciences, answers came easily in areas that had already been studied so the color was blue. Later, to avoid overlooking anything during study, we reviewed the material. Because it had already been set to memory in sociology studies, the color was blue. New material was remembered using the memorization method.

By November, the focus of all the students became studying for tests and reviewing past questions and solving them. And we reviewed the textbooks and used imagery to find better ways of learning. By December, the concentration became taking practice tests. We further examined the previous five years of questions and prepared for the tests in January. Due to the students being tense in January, there was some instability, but by February the tension was gone and we attained 100 percent success in the practice tests for entrance to Azabu Middle School. In April, admission to Azabu took place.

We can conclude from these results that right-brain training lessons necessary for study and entrance examinations have three very important pillars: (1) QSR, (2) image training, and (3) memorization. Further, we can see a causal relationship between the colors that emerge from the textbooks and the level of comprehension of the student. School score rankings correlate with the colors derived.

Freely Using All Three Parts of the Brain to Live Naturally

Next we will move on to how to communicate with one's inner self. By accessing deep areas of the diencephalon, our students are

The Three Pillars
- QSR
- Imagery
- (Long term) Memorization

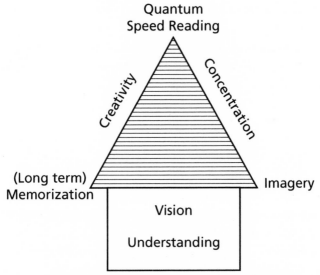

Quantum
Speed Reading

Creativity

Concentration

(Long term)
Memorization

Imagery

Vision

Understanding

Effortlessly connecting to the left brain

able not only to decide on the secondary school of their choice, but also to employ a method of learning that achieves their goal. As you can see in the illustration above, there is a three-tiered structure in our brains: the neocortex (primate brain), the archicortex, or old cortex (mammalian brain), and the brain stem (reptilian brain). All three tiers should be used absolutely to the fullest. By staying within the confines of regular left-brain learning, however, none of what we have described thus far would have been possible.

Making full use of this three-tiered brain structure is our natural way of living and, I believe we can say, a necessary orientation for adults and children alike. To date, the left brain has dominated personal development. It is the logic function that unfolds in speech, writes sentences, and makes calculations. And, of course, such ability is essential. It would make no difference how richly we used the imaging ability of the right brain if there were no left-brain ability to express it logically; we would have no way to communicate it. Unfortunately, our educational system is based on giving concrete form to thoughts and excludes any emphasis on right-brain abilities.

To be more whole, it is important for people who have already developed left-brain skills to try their best to develop the right brain. There is great fulfillment in fully activating all parts of the brain, including the left and right brains as well as the diencephalon. For young children, whose brains have not yet become fixed, it is harmful to be locked into solely left-brain thinking patterns. Surely, it is beneficial for children to embody the natural state of living before they are inducted into our left-brain systems.

Having Fun Studying Is the Key to Learning

I confidently tell my students that there is absolutely no reason why studying should be a cause of hardship. I tell them to relax and to learn how to have fun learning. I say that I will teach them how to do that. Studying should not be done with a solely selfish intent. Young T. G. said something of note: "I really have to use my nervous energy when trying to do Quantum Speed-Reading in order to feel the energy of the textbooks." He said that it is really easy and relaxing to do QSR on fiction stories, and not necessary to force the quantum information into flowing.

I have mentioned that the degree of difficulty in understanding something involves classifying the colors. Different colors are delicately emitted with subtle differences depending on the material. Using T. G. as an example again, he thought ratio problems in arithmetic were really hard for him. Contrary to his expectations, however, the color green emerged when doing one. He suddenly realized that he actually had a talent for ratio questions. This became the opportunity for him to start enjoying doing ratio problems, and he actually became very good at them.

The previous example shows how there can be a discrepancy

between everyday left-brain thinking and one's essential subconscious mind. In other words, by applying right-brain learning techniques, we can clearly see which study areas we are weak in and thus where to concentrate our study efforts.

3

The Uses of
Quantum Speed-Reading

Thinking it was just in my mind, I got ready to leave. Then I heard it again: "Take me home!" I thought, this is really weird. I looked around and there was the pot of flowers I had previously picked up.

Reinforcing Individuality
through Positive Suggestion

For elementary school students, one lesson at Shichida schools lasts 90 minutes. The first exercise is called *Relaxation Time*. We begin the lesson by releasing stress, and at the same time stimulating both the motor and sensory areas of the brain. Children walk across balance beams blindfolded and play running games. Then they lie on their sides and do deep breathing exercises, after which they are more open to suggestion. I believe this suggestibility is highly important.

An example of a positive reinforcement or suggestion is: "You are all really great, and just be the way you are," followed by "You don't have to do things like everybody else does; your own way is just fine." It is not about getting into competition with others, but rather about finding your own way of doing something and then going ahead and doing it.

We also make the children aware that the answers lie within them. Such suggestions encourage the children to develop individuality, and they begin to believe that the answers do indeed lie within them. It is a case of first acknowledging the children and making them more existentially aware. You may wonder why I work in this way. I do not want children to lose their moorings after they leave school, like a kite whose string breaks. I want to educate children so they are well grounded.

The Four Pillars of the Power of Suggestion

Suggestion	Power
1: You have wonderful ability.	Relates to innate ability
2: You are fine just as you are now. (It's great that you were born.)	Relates to issues of self-worth
3: It's OK not to be the same as everyone else. You have your own way of doing things.	Relates to individuality
4: The answers all lie within you.	Relates to the power of creative thinking

So the two important points are:

• Get out of the mold you have been in thus far and return to your primal, energetic self.
• Evoke the next new ability.

I want to educate children to be able eventually to see the essential elements of everything around them. This allows the stress that has built up in their bodies until that point, due to the principle of competition, to be released. The tension unwinds. With those children who have been de-stressed, we can give positive reinforcement such as: "Just having you here is great," "It's fine to do it in your own way," and "You have fantastic talents." With these messages, the stresses and strains that build up daily in them are rapidly dissolved. Then their individuality emerges. They are able to understand that the answers come from within them. If this way of thinking takes root in small children, there is no more need for them to be competitive. It becomes all right to live without always comparing themselves to others. I believe that these children will be able to perceive the essence of any situation and know what it is they really want to do, and also what needs to be done in any given situation.

I believe this type of education is incredibly important.

Talking with Our Subconscious Mind and to Our Cells

Our waking state of consciousness operates during the day and sleeps at night. But the subconscious mind works day and night. If we think, "I have got to do this or that," the subconscious will work while we sleep to achieve that goal. The subconscious mind tries to fulfill our wishes and desires, and we should be very thankful. We need to be extremely grateful and show consideration to our mind and our body, and even to our cells.

Our students have conversations with their own cells, and, in some cases, symptoms associated with atopic skin reaction and asthma have improved. First, they say to their cells, "Thanks for working for me day and night," and then they ask the cells what they would like them to do on their behalf. They can thus acquire specific information. The resulting "prescription" appears as an image that brings with it flashes of understanding. There have even been children who took action based on this information and were cured of asthma and atopic skin problems. [Translator's note: The latter, an irritable skin condition resembling eczema and called *atopy* in Japan, is almost epidemic in that country, with very little treatment to alleviate it.]

Thoughts Are Communicated to Flowers As Well

It started while I was working in a small classroom one day. There was a florist next door. In front of this florist's shop were potted flowering plants that had lost their petals and were being thrown out. I thought this was such a pity, and so I took one back to my classroom. The small pot was overflowing, and so I repotted the plant and left it in a spot with plenty of sun. Then on the last day of school before the traditional New Year holiday, I said my year-end farewells to students and teachers with the customary "See you again next year."

When it came time to head home, I heard something like "Take me home with you."

"Who's that?" I asked, turning around to see who was there, but there was nobody. Thinking it was just in my mind, I got ready to leave.

Then I heard it again: "Take me home!"

I thought, this is really weird. I looked around and there was the potted plant I had previously picked up. But, because my hands were full, I was unable to take the plant home with me. So I apologized to it, saying, "I'm so sorry. I'll give you plenty of water. Let's meet in the new year," and left it there.

I was busy during that New Year holiday and forgot about the plant. When I returned to work, it had completely wilted, even though I had given it plenty of water. I had to do something fast, so I took it straight home with me. I put it in my sunny living room and began to talk to it all the time. Then one morning, as I was getting ready to leave and was about to step out of the living room, I heard a voice in my mind saying, "Look at me, look at me!" Surprised, I turned around and saw that beautiful white flowers were blooming on the plant!

With Words, the Amaryllis Flowered

Other episodes like this occurred. I have an amaryllis plant on my veranda at home. Now there are plenty of flowers blooming, but in the past the plant would just produce leaves without any flowers.

At that time, I decided to speak to the amaryllis plant and said, "If it's not going to flower, then I'll just throw it out." Two or three days later, I was on a company trip in Kyoto. On returning home, the amaryllis plant on the veranda was full of buds. From that point, it just kept getting bigger and eventually produced flowers twice the normal size. Thus we can see that thought energy projected from the subconscious can affect plants as well as people.

Listening to Trees and Hearing of Future Events

At a certain point, my visits to Makoto Shichida's home in Shimane grew more frequent. Since it is not far from the great shrine at Izumo, I would go there to pray and ask that if this educational system was really important for children, it be divinely protected. As I was returning from one of these visits and was walking in a section of the inner grounds that has lots of trees, I heard one of the trees say, "OK, that will be enough now!" I wondered what this was about, but it turned out that my visits to Shimane abruptly stopped soon after that, due to outside circumstances.

I like trees and often go to visit the shrine near my home, where there are numerous 300-year-old ginkgo trees. Every time I go to pray there, I talk to the trees. This first began when I heard a tree there say, "Count to 30!" Even though I was hesitant, I did in fact count to 30. And then the weirdest thing happened. The pain I had in my back at that time disappeared.

Then later I heard from the trees, "There will be a new general manager put in charge and your business will improve quickly." That is exactly what happened.

The Four Special Functions of the Right Brain

There are four special functions of the right brain:

1. A resonance capability that is common to the vibrational frequencies of people and animate objects

2. An imaging capability that can quickly transform impressions into correlated images

3. A high-speed memorization capability that can instantaneously memorize troves of information

4. A high-speed automatic processing capability that handles huge amounts of information

The ability to memorize at a high speed derives from the right brain's photographic-like intuitive imagery function. The high-speed automatic processing could also be termed its computer ability. The law of quantity and quality conversion says that the larger the amount of data being inputted, the higher is the quality of its comprehension. Furthermore, it has been stated elsewhere that the brain is activated by its reception of incoming data, and that changes are generated within its learning ability when it outputs the data (from the book *Love Activates the Brain,* by Gen Matsumoto, published by Iwaba Shoten Kan).

As the door to the right brain swings open, abilities such as this are automatically activated.

Our Students Foresee Changes in DNA

One of the greatest characteristics of the right brain is that it does not acknowledge the concept of difficulty. There exist no rules in the QSR technique with expressions like "Because this is easy," "Because this is difficult," or "This is just about right." And it does not matter how young the child is. If we simply think or verbally express affirmations like "This kid is great!" or "This child is amazing!" it will, in fact, unleash that child's abilities.

The students did a QSR of Dr. Kazuo Murakami's book *The Code of Life,* published by Sunmark Publishing. This is an academic book about DNA research. What we wanted to learn in this "reading" of the book was, through combining QSR with imaging, what would become of DNA in the future. One child said, "If DNA research continues to progress quickly, we might be able to create dinosaurs." Another said that DNA research might change how humans continue to evolve, and that in the far future we might have a totally different physical form from our current one. This was accomplished by reading the vibration of the book in combination with the right brain's imaging function picking up scenes of the future.

The Automatic Translation Function

As the pages of a book are flipped through at high speed, the right brain's "computer" automatic processing function starts to operate by itself. Unlike conventional forms of speed-reading, using QSR allows one book to be completely read in a flash. In the process, the vibrations being emitted from the book are translated into colors or images that then become information. Foreign languages are automatically translated into Japanese (or the language of the reader) and written alphabets are made into pictures. Even with Japanese books, difficult kanji characters are automatically translated into phonetic katakana letters. We might say that this is a character-letter conversion function. Thus the brain's computer has an automatic translation function using imagery and character-letter conversion.

A Whole Life with Right-Brain Development

Quantum Speed-Reading started as speed-reading books for greater comprehension, but this, in fact, is only the beginning. It is necessary that QSR and its advanced functioning also have a broadly based relationship with one's lifestyle, health issues, study, and the choice of a profession. If this is accomplished, then it becomes possible to lead a life in a completely different manner. Until now, almost everyone has lived their lives centered in a left-brain way. I would like you to understand, however, that learning and using the right brain's expanded abilities is the ultimate aim of this technique and, through that, to discover new aspects of our jobs, studies, health, and daily life. But, first and foremost, the basis for all these advances is the ability to use the imaging function of the brain.

Communicating with Children Using Images

The following episode involves a young boy who is very bright and also very affectionate, but is prone to being unsettled and during class fidgets a lot. As we were about to do some image training one day, he was sitting in the classroom three rows from the front and looking around the room. At this point, I made an appeal to him via mental imaging, saying, "You must look straight ahead and listen to what the teacher is saying." In my mental image, he then nodded and said, "OK, I will." I wondered if this had actually happened or I had just imagined it. Later, when we had moved on to the next lesson, I said to the class, "In the last lesson, I sent one of you a mental image. Did you get it?" To which the boy replied, "Yes, I got it. That's why I am looking straight ahead and listening to you, and that's why I can remember the kanji." The same student also sometimes sends me mental images, but there are times when I get them and times when I don't. He will sometimes say to me, "Sensei [teacher], I tried so hard to send you those images, but you were completely unaware!"

Improving Daily Life with Quantum Speed-Reading

We have made a great variety of discoveries while developing the Quantum Speed-Reading system. One of those is that a great deal of information can be processed almost instantaneously. Another is that our students became kinder and more obedient. Could it be that the sentiment that to get smarter involves pushing others aside, that you study just for yourself, and that you only care about yourself is erroneous? Could it be that it is possible to get to the top without this left-brain type of effort? It is worthwhile noting that children using QSR become less competitive and more affectionate with each other. During QSR lessons, the children sit in a circle and read through 50 books or so in a ten- to 15-minute period. As mentioned previously, after the lesson, the children really take care of the books. The 50 books are placed properly in three big baskets, with care taken that they are in the right order. When I first observed this, I wondered, "What on Earth is this about?" So I asked the children, "Why is it you are being so careful with these books?"

The reply was "Because these books are like our pets, and it feels like they are important treasures. That's why we can't treat them roughly." As we progress, the students seem to get more and more kindhearted. We began to consider how these abilities could be used for the good of society and individuals. We found that being a faster reader or a having a better understanding of textbook content was no longer considered competitive. On further reflection, it became clear that QSR is associated with the three pillars of (1) understanding text content, (2) grasping the author's thoughts, and (3) activating your own thoughts on the subject. It is thus no wonder that the heart becomes more peaceful.

In short, this technique is at the root of developing our essential consciousness. It is not so much an issue of left- or right-brain training, but more of using QSR to unleash the essence of who we are as living beings. I have come to feel this sentiment working with the children day after day. As previously mentioned, children have been cured of atopic skin reactions and asthma, and, moreover, by stimulating the sensory areas of the right brain, their sensitivity is enhanced. As far as daily life is concerned, we have seen them become more efficient in day-to-day affairs, improve their ability to process information, and develop their agility. It is my belief then that using QSR brings constructive changes to all areas of daily life.

4

Quantum Speed-Reading for Adults

Unlike the left-brain, with which we gradually learn through the piling up of information over a long period of time, the right brain creates a direct pathway to a corresponding understanding in about three months.

Linking Right-Brain Ability to the Left Brain

All human beings have the kind of right-brain ability cited in this opening statement. In order for this ability to take form, however, it needs to be connected to the left-brain circuits. Without continuing the training in speaking and writing, this right-brain pathway or circuit will atrophy and the abilities it enables will remain unused. As an example, when kindergarten pupils are compared with elementary and high-school students who have returned from abroad, the kindergarten children speak English much more fluently than the others. After two or three months, however, they lose their English-speaking ability. In point of fact, when my son attended a Spanish-speaking kindergarten, he spoke Spanish and was able to sing a variety of songs in that language. And yet, as soon as he entered a regular Japanese elementary school, that faculty disappeared. Students who study English in elementary and secondary schools do not lose their English-speaking ability. Therefore, it seems very important to establish these pathways properly in the left and right brains early on. By firmly fixing them, the pathways will not close up but should be freely available for the right brain to utilize even in adulthood.

The Reason It Is Difficult for Adults to Use Imagery

The greatest reason why adults are not easily able to master QSR is that they have lived their lives based on left-brain ways of thinking, and it is extremely difficult for them to change. Since every aspect of modern society has been created from left-brain thinking, utilizing the subconscious in itself becomes the central issue. One example would be how we read books by following the words. Using right-brain imagery to read books, we do not trace one word after another. So, if one is considering the opening up of these right-brain abilities, I think it is necessary to change at the very root how we conduct our daily lives. For one thing, we can have fun using the QSR imagery while reevaluating the way we go about doing things. It has been noted that we use but a fraction of our brain's true abilities in normal day-to-day life. Therefore, let's try to use them to the greatest extent.

Even Adults Can Do Quantum Speed-Reading

At designated schools around Japan, we conducted training in QSR. What was amazing was how quickly the students were able to do QSR. After two or three years of working with children, we came to understand that adults, too, can do QSR. All adults were once children with those same innate abilities. In the human brain-wave spectrum is a concentration suitable for learning; these waves are called *theta waves*. Children have especially high levels of theta-wave emissions. Scientifically, theta waves are lower in frequency than alpha waves, having a wavelength of about 3.5 to 7 hertz. It is likely that children are able to develop this right-brain facility because of higher levels of theta waves.

So would it not then be simply a matter of guiding adults to increase their theta-wave levels? For that, deep breathing training and what we call *Stick Image Training* are required. The stick image is fully explained in a later chapter, but for now, to put it simply, the body is imagined to have its muscles tensed as hard as a stick. Then the tension is suddenly released, and we return to normal. This is done via imagery only. We imagine that we are getting taut and then release the tension. This technique allows us to lower the frequency of our brain waves.

We held a "Right-Brain Seminar for Adults" a dozen or more times and included QSR training. We attempted to lower the brain-wave frequency of the participants during those seminars by using the deep breathing and rod imagery techniques. As a result, the adults perceived colors coming from the books and received images from them as well as messages. I noted that it took longer for the adults to complete these lessons than it did for the children, and the images they picked up were fainter. But, in the end, the adults, too, were able to perform Quantum Speed-Reading.

Right-Brain Circuits Can Be Created in Three Months

Right-brain abilities are not slowly nurtured like the left brain's building-up process. In fact, the new neural pathway can be created in about three months. In order to accomplish this in adult students, however, what becomes necessary are frequent and intense practices. Simply put, the key is single-minded training and a single-minded aim to use QSR. This is how the adult's right-brain ability gets activated. By contrast, when training children, it is important to have fun and treat it like a game to make sure they do not get bored. In this way, the limbic system (deep brain structures associated with learning, emotion, and memory) and the diencephalon can receive the necessary stimulation.

Astonishing Results from Right-Brain Development

Let's look at some of the results that have been experienced by those participating in the adult training seminars. A business seminar lasting four hours per lesson was held for three days straight. After it was completed, we heard people's various impressions. These can be divided into the following categories:

1. Health improvement
2. The development of precognitive ability
3. Memory improvement
4. Intuition development
5. Wish fulfillment
6. Improvement in timing
7. Improved concentration
8. Imaging power
9. Improvement in human relations and consideration for others
10. Feelings of stability
11. Life changes

The following data were collected from questionnaires. The following is a sampling of some of the delighted responses participants provided in each category.

1. Health Improvement

We have already seen how in children atopic skin reactions and general physical health improved after QSR. Similar effects were also noted by the adults.

- Sleeping duration was shortened. Some were able to sleep very soundly for shorter time periods.
- One person, who had a cold and was coughing a lot, continuously used imagery to stop it. He was then able to finish the seminar without coughing.
- Atopy was cured.
- Dieting efficacy was greatly improved.
- Body condition improved.

2. The Development of Precognitive Ability

We learned through the experiences of children doing QSR that their precognitive ability awakens. Adults reported the same phenomenon.

- A foreknowledge of events about to happen occurred quite often. In one case, someone thinking that it might be better to stay home was later caught for speeding.
- Being able to have an accurate presentiment increased. One participant received a book from a friend days after seeing an image of one of its pages during meditation.
- Other reports included being able to find a book in a bookstore more quickly and getting phone calls from people whose faces have just come into mind.
- While not thinking about anything in particular, an image would appear in the mind and later an incident connected to that image occurred.
- Something imagined would later manifest in reality.

3. Memory Improvement

One of the greatest effects of QSR training noted among adults was memory improvement and better memorization skills. They reported:

- Greater ease in remembering numbers
- Having very real dreams and being able to remember them vividly after waking up

- Being able to learn people's names more quickly
- Remembering hundreds of favorite scenes daily; and as this continued, three months later feeling a great sense of joy
- Daily practice of memorizing pi to ten more decimal places and being amazed at how much had been remembered

4. Intuition Development

Without a shadow of a doubt, intuition improves. As it does, so does the sense of judgment. Participants reported:

- Better intuition
- Improvement of hunches
- Ability to read more quickly the emotion behind facial expressions
- Getting the right score in advance for the World Cup match and guessing the sales total at a store before purchases were rung up
- Not being able to find something and then remembering upon waking from sleep where it was left
- An increase in intuitive judgment while talking to people
- A feeling of heading in the right direction after paying attention to flashes of insight

5. Wish Fulfillment

When it comes to wish fulfillment, an ability akin to psychokinesis appears. The adults reported:

- Being able to land a concert ticket that is really hard to obtain
- An increase in lottery wins
- When a desire to return to a former job arises, it seems more likely that such a position is available
- Finding something lost, getting something wished for, and events consciously envisioned beginning to occur
- Work going better; for example, without advertising, student enrollment increasing
- The faster the speed of thoughts, the faster they manifest in reality
- Things going more smoothly; places one desires to visit and events one wants to participate in work out well

- Achievements previously thought unattainable start to happen
- Without any negative effects on others, a feeling that things are taking shape joyfully is experienced
- Using imagery for playing golf, the nine-hole score comes out at 39 strokes, besting the previous low of 45
- At the year-end party raffle, one received the desired prize after firmly believing that this would happen
- In the workplace, after thinking of a person one wants to work with, that person joins in on the job; and conversely, the individual one prefers not to work with somehow isn't part of it
- After thinking that it would be better if a certain person did something, that is what happens
- Money that had been lent out was repaid
- When a pet cat went astray, everybody did a visualization exercise together and found it. Wishes come true through the use of strong imagery.

6. Improvement in Timing

In work as well as in human relationships, the right timing is an important factor. Many people experienced an improvement in timing, reporting:

- Useful information or books coming across one's path
- Not getting caught at traffic lights while driving
- Being more on time in general
- Becoming more in synch with right timing in situations in all areas of daily life
- Becoming more adept at planning events
- Being more positive about doing one's job, and work just starting to roll in
- Feeling that realizations needed for one's growth are happening more often

7. Improved Concentration

One of the results of using QSR is that concentration improves.

- The ability to concentrate at work grows, and there is more aware-ness of when one is having a flash of insight.
- Book-reading speed increases.
- There is more of an inclination to read, and the number of books read increases.

8. Imaging Power

QSR, as a matter of course, greatly increases imaging ability.

- Ideas pop into the mind more readily.
- Being able to hold an event in just the way imagined, and with favorable weather, occurs routinely.
- The envisioned image is as clear and sharp as a photograph.
- At work, good ideas flash into the mind much more often; designs and the colors needed effortlessly come to mind.
- Artistic appreciation and sensibility become much broader.
- The images in dreams are recalled more clearly.
- At work, the ability to see how things fit in a system begins to occur.
- Envisioning the contents of a book in the images of QSR occurs.
- By repetition of the residual image training, one's own imaging power increases.
- One becomes able to see colors using imaging.
- By imaging one's affairs at the start of each day, and then later reflecting on the day's events, it is often the case that the events play out as perceived.

9. Improvement in Human Relations and Consideration for Others

The heart is enriched, one becomes capable of greater consid-eration for others, and, because cooperation and harmony are learned, many adult participants in the QSR seminars commented that human relationships improved. This was especially true in the case of family relationships. Participants reported:

- Hoping for the best for others or a particular individual becoming the pattern

- Not being as easily angered as in the past
- Having less feeling of haste and more of a sense of composure
- Family bonds getting stronger
- Becoming more kindly disposed to all people, especially in one's family
- The family atmosphere becoming harmonious; improved family relationships
- Being able to forgive people and to look at human relations from a broader perspective
- Not usually experiencing a negative change with people
- An increase in being asked to help people

10. Feelings of Stability

Being aware of one's own sense of stability increases with QSR. This involves a reduction of stress and being able to act with a sense of calm in daily life, reported as follows:

- Even if a surprising event catches one unawares, one can go about one's business unfazed
- Being able to feel relaxed, even when serving guests, and seeing an improvement in the way one carries through on things
- In the workplace, there is far less hesitation and a clearer sense of judgment
- Having the ability to see a way out, even in difficult situations
- A change in negative emotions and a feeling of being more genial
- The ability to switch from one mood to another mood speeds up
- Stress reduction
- Even while doing image training on a train, the mind is at peace
- Feelings are much more composed
- There is more emotional tolerance
- There is a greater ability to think things through slowly

11. Life Changes

If such previously noted changes are occurring, then the whole sense of life itself will be greatly altered, as participants reported:

- The personality gets brighter and every day becomes more enjoyable
- One is better able to accept oneself even when being negative
- The way of thinking becomes much more positive
- One is able to handle normally things that were previously shocking
- There is the ability to turn a loss into a gain at work, when a problem is turned into a positive situation
- Decisions are made faster and with no worry associated with them.
- Actions are carried out faster
- Good things seem to be happening, and wishes are fulfilled with a sense that one's happiness is increasing
- The joy of being alive is sensed stronger than previously
- There is less mental irritation, and people say that one's attitude is far less abrasive than in the past
- One is more mentally relaxed and experiences a sharpening of the sixth sense
- Images of a much brighter future are envisioned along with its possibilities and a growing belief in oneself. By clearly imaging an objective, one is now able to complete it.
- The mind works more sharply

So, as we have seen, there are countless benefits to using QSR.

5

The Methodology
of QSR Training

A really intriguing phenomenon occured at that point. A light blue sky and orange flames appeared in the image and, seeing this, one child said, "From now on, the air and fire are going to be more important."

Thus far we have noted the benefits gained from QSR training in both adults and children. No doubt the reader has now developed an interest in QSR. So let's look at the actual training. The three key steps of Quantum Speed-Reading, when broadly divided into categories, are:

1. Image training
2. Eye training
3. Rapid page-flipping

These steps are the foundation of QSR. In addition, if we add the two ancillary techniques of *Afterimage Training* and *"The Place of the Heart,"* we encompass the five main points of the training. (When you begin to practice QSR, imagery can sometimes appear as real as if it were actually observed physical phenomena. There are also cases where it evokes similar sensations like smell. In the spectrum of imagery generated by the right brain, the most accessible are dream images. When it comes to measuring the development of right-brain abilities, we start by asking if the person dreams in color or in black and white. By persevering in right-brain training, we do begin to dream in color.)

Image Training
Afterimage (Residual Image) Training

Practicing Afterimage Training in artificial light or natural sunlight or by using orange training cards results in the residual images (images retained after turning off a light or closing one's eyes) tending to last increasingly longer. Further, we are soon able to see afterimages in primary colors almost unconsciously. In the beginning, even when using orange training cards, the images tend to be in secondary colors. When using a blue card, for example, the afterimage tends to be in orange. With further training, however, it makes no difference what color is used: The afterimages are in the correct color. The next step is to use round cards and to visualize them as being square or triangular. When this is accomplished, imagery is freely accessible to the mind.

Eye Training
Evoking Images

Before commencing QSR, we conduct eye muscle training, simply called *Eye Training*, to expand the visual field. The eyeball is moved up and down and then left to right, with each position being held for ten seconds. The upper and lower oblique muscles of the eye are trained. Doing this at high speed, we can begin to sense colors and light. For example, stars may appear in the middle of an image, or butterfly shapes or even square shapes. This type of training facilitates a faster entry to QSR. Though it may be difficult in the beginning, it is a good idea to move the eyes as rapidly as possible. From this starting point with colors and light, the right brain's five senses awaken. We begin to feel a dazzling sensation, warm feelings, as well as smells and sensations of discomfort. Through the repetition of this training, the sensory faculties of the right brain start to surface. Though you might consider this as QSR ability, it is still only the preparatory stage of upper and lower oblique muscle training for the eyes. By rhythmically training the eyes at high speeds, we can evoke images with light, color, and form. These prepare us for QSR.

At this stage, we have succeeded in evoking images of the wind, the sea, clouds, earth, and rain. At times, the sensory perceptions are stimulated and involve feeling a gentle wind, a salty sea, cold clouds, soft earth, and wet rain. These sensations appear as images and, at the same time, sounds are perceivable. The wind whooshes by, the sea crashes, the clouds swish, the earth crunches, and the rain patters. The following are comments made by children who were doing eye training:

"Doing this made me feel relaxed. Then my whole mood brightened up."

"It is a strange feeling doing this. It seems like light is shining down on me."

Here we can see that the individuality of each of the children is being expressed. We next did eye training by using a physics textbook. A really intriguing phenomenon occurred at that point. A light blue sky and orange flames appeared in the image and, seeing this, one child said, "From now on, the air and fire are going to be more important." So, even though we are only doing simple eye training, there is some meaning contained in the colors and the light that appear during practice. Furthermore, it is not only colors and light that manifest, but also sounds and other sensations. All of the sense perceptions of the right brain are set in motion.

3D Training

The eyes and the right brain are profoundly connected. One theory holds that three-dimensional (3D) vision is related to the midbrain within the brain stem. Because the midbrain is "the heart and mind center," staring at images in 3D can at times evoke powerful feelings in the heart. From this experience, we can see how the eyes, the brain, and the heart seem to be connected. When practicing 3D exercises, we often use images from nature or mandala patterns. With eye training exercises, because of a direct link to the right brain, colors and light are perceived. Eye training involves the training of the eye muscles utilizing the three techniques of image training, eye training, and rapid page flipping. Though doing only these exercises can lead to seeing colors and light, their practice alone does not easily lead to the success experienced by our students. It is therefore important to increase the speed of each exercise. Using a method called the *Camera Shutter,* which involves blinking rapidly during eye training, it becomes easier to see colors and light.

Artificial Light Training

Artificial Light Training involves using an ordinary lamp stand with a 30-watt red, green, or yellow bulb, if possible. (It is very important to be able to see the images in color.) This lamp stand is positioned about six feet away from the individual and switched off after that person stares at it for 30 seconds. Then the starer looks at the afterimage that remains behind the eyelids. This afterimage training is most important as a basis for seeing internal images. Next, we practice breathing exercises, using abdominal breathing with the eyes gently closed. Another name for this is *hara* or *tanden* (*tantien* in Chinese) breathing.

Stick Image Training

Because relaxation and concentration are important for image work, we train in tensing and letting go repeatedly. We call this *Stick Image Training*. At the beginning, we regulate breathing and loosen up the body. Then we stiffen up the whole body as if it were a stick, and loosen up completely again. This gets repeated three times. This kind of pretraining has the effect of shifting our unconscious left-brain way of living and coaxing us into a more right-brain mode. That is done with breathing and with the stick or rod imagery. This is then linked to the afterimage training used to visualize images. For children, this kind of training is quite simple, but it can indeed be difficult for adults. Because we have spent most of our lives centered on left-brain activity, without creating the right mental alignment, it seems very difficult to access the right brain.

Rapid Page Flipping

How to Evoke Colors with Quantum Speed-Reading

Adults have a deeply ingrained habit of following the printed word when flipping through the pages of a book. As a means of breaking this habit, there is a way of flipping through a book with the eyes blindfolded. Even with a blindfold, if pretraining has been done with the orange card system, the colors will clearly become visible. Once this has happened, the next step is to grasp their meaning. It then becomes relatively easy to comprehend the substance of books by repeatedly taking off the blindfold and confirming the visible colors.

Quite often during the blindfold training, images that have nothing to do with the content of the book are evoked. This indicates that, within the three-tiered system of the brain, the zone of the right brain has not been exclusively reached; there is a bleed-through from the left to right brain. For that reason, even if something is clearly perceived, there is a comprehension gap between that and what would be accessed by the more essential aspects of right-brain consciousness.

When one is able to do QSR with a blindfold, the next step is to remove it and to evoke colors through high-speed page-flipping. Though the final objective is to perceive images without the blindfold, it is necessary to do quite a lot of training to reach that stage.

Books Applicable to Quantum Speed-Reading

Books are easier or more difficult to access at the quantum vibrational level, depending on their content. First, easily accessed books are those in which the author has been very clear in his or her assertions. When an author has forcefully expressed his or her beliefs about an ideology, for example, I believe it is that much easier to grasp the content of the book. Second, books that have common themes about nature can also be strongly perceived, because we are living beings with interests above and beyond the human realm. Examples of such books might be those about plants, animals, oceans, or mountains. Third, books related to one's own field of interest are also easily accessible. When choosing books to be used for QSR training, it is better to start with books in these categories. Furthermore, flipping through books whose content is already known is another good method of evoking the colors and images. In this way, we can get accustomed to picking up the messages coming from the books and the best speed at which pages should be flipped.

Staring Practice with Patterns and Words

Staring Practice is a training system that involves staring at a pattern or series of words and then accessing the mental images evoked. In terms of patterns, it is best to use those that reflect symbolic images such as mandalas or patterns in nature. When it comes to words, we can use "ANT," for example, and by staring at the word, images will come to mind. Through the repetition of such training, we are able to envision an ant perched on top of a leaf or ants carrying food. If the word is "BIRTH" and the individual is a woman, she would perhaps envision the birth of her own child. In short, the word elicits images.

Although our right brain contains a great deal of information, it is difficult to access it. The reason is that it surfaces to the imagery level with great difficulty. There are times, however, when it does just pop up and that is when the right conditions and the environment are present. For example, let's imagine that you are at a friend's graduation ceremony. What surfaces out of the right brain's inputted information might be images of your own child's graduation ceremony. This implies that if the right conditions are present, then we can always access such imagery. With that in mind, training that uses words for recollection can act in the same way as a conduit between the right brain and left brain.

Training Requires Intensity, Frequency, and Continuation

QSR training is not about spending hours a day practicing. What become necessary are the three pillars of intensity, frequency, and continuation. What is important then is to continue training for three months to the best of your ability in terms of daily time. Don't decide beforehand how many hours you will train per day. The reason is that the left brain will from that point on click into action. Rather than driving yourself with a rigid schedule, it would be better to continue the training while enjoying it.

Generally speaking, the period for this training requires three months. This is the minimal time needed to create right-brain pathways. As noted previously, the left brain creates its pathways through a process of building up, and so the resultant number of circuits will be relative to the length of training. The right brain, however, does not build on what has been learned in a linear fashion, but rather in parallel or lateral circuits. The right-brain "channels" thus opened up can later in life become stronger or weaker, but if they are used on an ongoing basis, they will never become disconnected. From that point of view, this is similar to learning to ride a bicycle.

Time, Space, and Distance Are Irrelevant

The preceding information has been concerned with the methodology of beginners' training. When it comes to intermediate students, it is no longer about just understanding the book in hand. At this stage, you will be able to access QSR imagery from beyond the linear space-time matrix, such as calling up images of distant and unknown locations and buildings, for example. Using the QSR training, information about such places can be accessed. Since abilities of this nature do crop up with training, I will briefly explain it here.

In the students' classes, after they had easily mastered how to do QSR on general books, they went on to apply QSR techniques beyond the constraints of time and space. First, we had them create images of Stanford University. At this point in their training, they were quite accustomed to the lessons and thus evoked images in great detail. In fact, although the students had never seen Stanford University, the characteristics found in their images matched up well with the actual site. Here was a tennis court, there a broad hallway, in such and such a place there were books in a library, and so on. They were specific about the location of buildings, and I was rather shocked to see photographs of Stanford and realize their images were exactly the same.

We then had them create images of picking up a book at the university library, reading it, and understanding its content. The children were able to tell what kinds of books were in the library at Stanford, that there were a lot of specialized research books. On imaging Harvard University, they were able to see a great many books devoted to improving society. Later, we had the children look at Lao Tzu's literature or review what the Wright brothers had written. They were able to do this freely. In this way, we were able to determine that the QSR technique was not in any way restricted by space and time.

Information Can Be Obtained Even from Blank Book Pages

If we can step outside of the time and space framework, then why not, as a further step, get information from nothing? We had students flip through the pages of a blank book we had entitled "Personal History, My Own Birth." The result was seeing scenes from the individual's birth and personal history. This included seeing oneself covered in blood at birth or being cuddled by one's father. Their parents later confirmed these impressions as accurate; this was not just a child's fantasy. Flipping through another blank book, entitled "Rare Insects of the World," resulted in one of the students seeing a rare insect. He reported seeing a green ladybug on the white cover of the book. I do not know anything about insects, but there happened to be a boy in the class who was a "bug professor," and he confirmed that such an insect does exist. So one can obtain a lot of different information using this blank-book technique, which we did repeatedly. This is not only about the right-brain extension, but also about connecting with a level of reality even more profound.

Blank Book Pages as Complementary Material for Clearer Imaging

Using the blank book as a catalyst for QSR to reach that sphere of imagery beyond space and time limitations is called *Image Quantum Speed-Reading*. After using imagery to access information about a specific situation, we then went on to choose a theme to use with a blank book. An example would be "the big bang." Flipping through the pages of a blank book, with the imagined title of "The Big Bang," resulted in the appearance of images of the big bang. These images came with written explanations. Rather than simply seeing the imagery, we used a blank book as a catalyst to produce very specific and detailed information.

Next, when we thought that we could also learn about history by flipping through the blank pages of a book, all of the history from the ancient past to the present became available in these blank white pages. It would be fair to say that the blank-book technique makes the images far clearer and that this is a complementary tool to obtaining written explanations. For example, when a student is composing a poem, that student can use the blank book and see the words of the poem. All he or she needs to do then is copy them down.

Adults, in particular, find it easier to evoke images using a blank book, rather than expecting them to form by suggestion only. Of course, the written explanations for our students appeared at this point in Japanese with the difficult kanji characters revealed in the hiragana phonetic script. The right-brain computer automatically converts the characters.

"Flying In" to Read without Turning the Pages

There are two ways to do QSR. One of them is the previously discussed way of flipping through the pages of a book. In addition, there is a way called *Flying In*. In this, you use imagery to miniaturize yourself and enter another person's body or a book, and from there perform a procedure or access information. Through applying this QSR technique, we can enter a human body to heal disease, or leap inside an apple to find out how many seeds it contains, or inside a stone or soil to obtain images. This technique changes your own physical particles into waves and allows you to "fly" on those quantum waves. For example, you could put a book inside a paper bag and then "fly in." Your miniaturized self would get inside the book and cover itself with glue. Then you would roll over the pages in your images and "pick up" the contents of the pages through your skin! This is a method akin to ESP remote viewing. It is a way of speed-reading without turning the pages of a book. Compared to the page-flipping, the QSR flying-in technique accesses more information and is able to reach deeper parts of the diencephalon. This method is still in the developmental stages, however, and in areas such as the improvement of learning skills there are certain difficulties with its use. Next, we are going to acquire more information through this quantum vibration by freely using our computer-like abilities.

We all sit together in a circle and read about 50 books in a few minutes.

This is a picture of a crayfish
drawn from imagery work.

Flipping through the book, colors change into images.

Light green and blue colors are being emitted from the book.

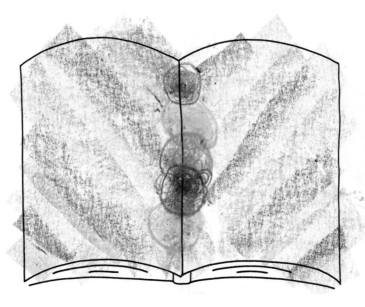

Light rainbow colors are being emitted.

宇宙人のいる教室

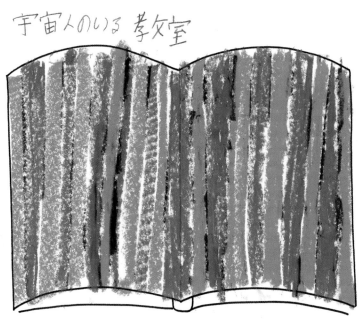

Sometimes striped colors are emitted.

とびだせ
ズッコケ事件記者

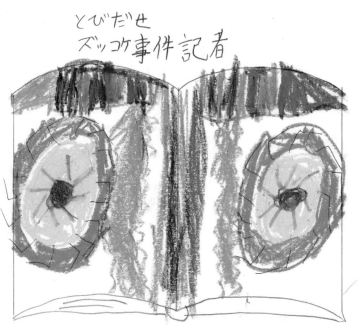

Color and shape take form.

When eye training is speeded up, colors, light, and forms are emitted.

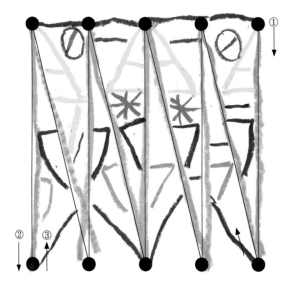

When color and light are emitted, we can then do speed reading.

The right brain's abilities are enhanced when color and form appear.

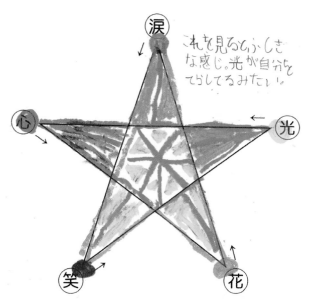

これを見ると、ふしぎ
な感じ。光が自分を
てらしてるみたい。

If we use letters in eye training, sense perceptions
accompany the images.

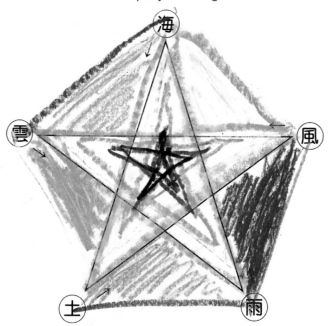

Using letters in eye training, the five senses are
stimulated and something akin to QSR occurs.

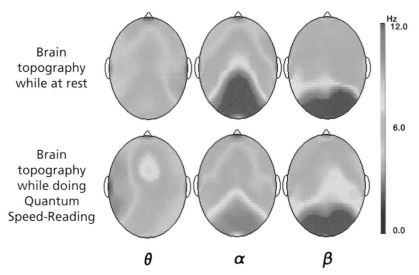

| | θ | α | β |

Brain topography while at rest

Brain topography while doing Quantum Speed-Reading

Hz
12.0

6.0

0.0

(Above) Resting state brain topography during speed reading. This brain topography was taken in August of 2001 on T. G. at Japan Medical University by Dr. Kimiko Kawano. We can see that theta waves are being emitted from the central frontal area when concentrating and doing QSR. This type of brain wave is appropriate for study and it appears in the front and central area of the head (about the middle of the area between crown and forehead) continuously.

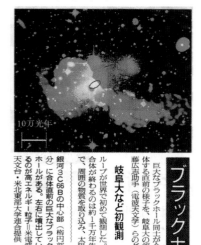

(Left) The Asahi newspaper report from May 23, 2003, along with *Science* magazine, confirms that there are many kinds of black holes, as noted by our young student K.

Flipping through the pages of an English book, this student can understand the contents through the Japanese and the imagery which it "emits."

Students see colors, light, and imagery as well as perceive smells and sounds from the books.

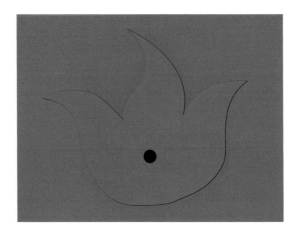

The campfire: Stare at the top black dot for 30 seconds and then look at the bottom one. You will see the faint traces of a red fire above the logs. If you carry on looking you will clearly see this. If you do not, breathe in slowly and once more start staring at the green flame and begin all over.

The orange card: This is training so as to be able to visualize images. Try staring at this for 30 seconds without blinking.

The 3D stereogram:
The field of pansies.
Along with the butter-
flies that have flown
here attracted by the
scent what else can
you see?

Circles are born from within circles. Turn the page sideways and see
two mandalas become one.

The seven colors of the rainbow. Do afterimage training beginning from the red down.

Dates / Subj.	9 13	9 20	9 27	10 4	10 18	10 25	11 8	11 15	11 22	11 29	12 6	12 13	12 20	1 24	1 31	2 1
Japanese																
Math																
Science																
Social Science																
Ranking	17	17	17	17	4	2	3	2	2	11	2	6	3			
Name of school visualized			Azabu										Azabu and university	Pass or fail entrance test		

QSR and exam preparation

We had the students QSR the textbooks of prep schools. Here, you can see the colors perceived and their relationship with prep school rankings.

After doing the QSR, a student is drawing
the colors that the book emitted.

These girls are doing the same.

6

Practical Training

By implementing this method to move into the realm of imagery, even adults will be able to see inner images, their intuition will blossom, and they will be able to pick up the messages coming out of books.

Let's begin the practice of QSR with an introduction to the children's program. The actual step-by-step instructions are in chapter 10, and all the pictures referred to are in the color section.

The Training Program for Children
Step 1: Image and Eye Training

Staring Practice

Keep your breathing rhythmic while you look at the word "flower." As you breathe out, you get farther away and as you breathe in you get closer to the word "flower." What kinds of images come up?

Afterimage Training

Look at the picture of a campfire. Stare at the black dot in the middle of the green fire for 30 seconds, and then shift your focus to the lower black dot. You will be able to see a red fire dimly above the firewood.

3D Stereogram

Here you can see a field of pansies. Look at the purple dots at the bottom and you will see a peculiar shape surfacing as if something were flying toward you.

Eye Training

(Use the diagrams in chapter 10.) Start with up and down movements of the eyes. Follow rapidly the direction of the arrows in the diagrams with your eyes. You can use a metronome to gradually speed up the tempo. Then proceed to the left/right arrow sequences. And then do the up/diagonal/down eye exercises. Imagine the Earth moving to wind, clouds, and rain. How did it go? Were you able to hear the crashing of the sea, the sound of the rain, or sense its smell? Once you get accustomed to doing these exercises, please check to see if any colors are visible. Look at the colors the children have painted in their pictures. Try painting the colors that you perceive.

Step 2: Flying In

Flying in entails the use of breathing techniques and a simple meditation where you can go into your own body, or "fly in" to a book. First, try flying in to your body and then in to a book.

Step 3: Relaxation-Concentration-Envisioning

Rod or Stick Image Training

Lie down and breathe long, shallow breaths, and then envision yourself as a rod or a stick.

Artificial Light Training

Set a lamp stand with a naked bulb about 6.5 feet away from you and select a book you have never read. Next, look at the light bulb for a few seconds, and then close your eyes. The image of the light will probably appear between your eyes. While keeping that image in view, you then fly in to the book and "read" the contents. You can specify a page number, then afterward look on that page in the book to confirm what is written there.

Step 4: Staring Practice and Afterimage Practice

After you have finished the eye training, lie down and do long, shallow breathing. Following this exercise, do the rod imaging, the artificial light practice, and then QSR with a blindfold on. (This is where you are blindfolded and speed-read the book by seeing colors and images and also grasping any messages.)

Eye Training for Adults

These exercises relate to the usual set routines we do when training children in QSR. If you can proceed as far as step 4, then it becomes quite possible to do QSR well. Although it appears that children, having few preconceptions, can master it quickly, we still use the same system to train adults. With them, we also begin with afterimage training, using the basic observation of artificial light sources, and then the orange card techniques. We next use eye training to evoke light and colors, and here is where it begins to take a lot of time when working with adults. Here is where we introduce the "camera shutter" training, which involves blinking the eyes rapidly, so the brain can no longer distinguish if the eyes are open or closed. This allows visual imagery to occur even with the eyes closed. In this exercise, it is important to keep the speed of blinking as fast as possible. Another technique is doing eye training with the eyes open followed by training with them closed. Through the introduction of these image-training methods, even adults can see pictures, improve their intuitive capabilities, and grasp the meaning of the books.

The Training Program for Adults

The questionnaire called "The Child Power Test for Adults" is a method to calibrate the skills you need to do QSR. The higher your

Child Power score, the easier it will be for you to do QSR. If you score low, however, there is no need to be despondent about it. Through this training, you should be able to improve your Child Power.

Step 1: Image and Eye Training

The Staring Practice, Afterimage Training, and 3D Stereogram exercises are the same as the ones for children.

For the Eye Training, first visualize colors, for example, red, yellow, and green. If simply visualizing the colors alone is difficult, visualize the red color of an apple, the yellow of a lemon or banana, and the green of a watermelon. The next step is to visualize being outside and going to the front door of your house. Then find out what is happening at your house now. Or, if you happen to be at home right now, then visualize going to a close friend's front door and find out what is happening at his or her house. Who is there? What are they doing? The important point about this exercise is to confirm the facts. For example, if you visualized someone coming to visit your home, call and find out if you were correct.

Step 2: Flying In

This is done in the same way as in the children's practice: flying in to your own body and flying in to fruit.

To fly in to a specific book, use a book about which you know nothing. The practice involves relaxing, then concentrating, and after that visualizing. First, lie down and breathe slowly, then do the rod or stick imaging. Next, do the artificial light training and proceed to "fly in" to the book. As in the children's program, you "fly in" to a particular page and then afterward check what is written there.

Step 3: Staring and Afterimage Practice

First, do the eye training, followed by lying down, breathing slowly, and doing the rod or stick image exercise. Then do the artificial light training. Next, blindfold your eyes and then proceed with QSR. From the book, you can get messages, colors, and imagery. Can you grasp what the author was thinking and feeling?

7

Simple Applications
for Daily Life

One part of it was lit up with a fuzzy kind of white. I figured out that this meant empty seats, and so I boarded that train car. There was indeed an empty seat.

Applying the Training to Daily Life at Your Own Enjoyable Pace

How did you fare? Did you manage to memorize the training targets? I would like to suggest that you practice for a few minutes every day. You may find it hard to make progress in the beginning; however, this is more about getting accustomed to practicing than it is about learning something. You will no doubt be surprised when you realize that you do have the power to do QSR. Some people find it easier than others to develop these skills. Those who find it easier are not stressed out and/or fixated on one approach. As a result, they are able to see inner imagery relatively easily. Or, to put it another way, the ability to step outside the left brain when required is in itself the

"Child Power," the ability to understand information with one's sensibility and feelings. For people who believe that the left brain is sufficient for all learning, this may be difficult to accept at first.

It is important, therefore, to enjoy the lessons and not be concerned with succeeding at these practices. A crucial point, especially in the case of adults, is that they should proceed at their own pace, not compare themselves with others and become fixated on results.

Predicting Empty Seat Locations on Trains

The basis of QSR is inner imaging. Therefore, it is vital that we continue training in order to see the inner images. Because you will get more and more frustrated if you try too hard to see them, please treat this exercise as simply playing a game. Approaching it as a game offers a shortcut to opening up the development of the right brain. Here is one training method that makes this just such a game. Let's say you are on your way home from work, and you are tired as you head for the commuter train. Anybody would want to get a seat in this situation. No self-respecting adult, however, would get into a struggle over an empty seat. Instead, you can use precognition. Imagine the train coming in and visualize the passengers on it.

When I first did this exercise, an image surfaced of the people on the train; they looked like round balls. One part of it was lit up with a fuzzy kind of white. I figured out that this meant empty seats, and so I boarded that train car. There was indeed an empty seat. Of course, it could have been just a coincidence, so the next day I did the same thing. Sure enough, I found another empty seat. On the following day, there were two fuzzy white areas lit up, but when I boarded, those two seats were taken. At the next station, however, the people in those seats got off the train and I was able to take a seat.

Because this is a relatively elementary step in imaging, I believe it is possible for beginners to accomplish. Even though this is QSR training, you can do it in a relaxed manner without driving yourself too hard.

Condensing Sleep Time with Imagery

Because the Japanese are so busy, we often reduce the amount of time we sleep. Thus many of us would like a method to condense sleeping time if at all possible. This exercise does just that via a kind of self-hypnosis using inner imagery. It involves self-suggestion. Just before going to sleep, you repeat a pattern of tensing and relaxing your body. Then you plant the self-suggestion: "In the morning, I have slept soundly for eight hours, and all the tiredness has left me, so I wake up bright-eyed and bushy-tailed." In this way, the subconscious is programmed, so even if you actually sleep for only six hours, it will feel like eight hours of solid sleep. It really does condense sleeping time and you still awake refreshed. This is one example of many QSR techniques that can be applied to everyday life.

A Technique for Morning Flashes of Inspiration

There is also a way to summon morning flashes of inspiration. Before going to sleep at night, if you program the subconscious with the idea, "Tomorrow morning I want some insights about such and such a situation," when you wake up the following day, there will be a shower of ideas. It is therefore a good idea to have a notebook and pencil at hand in order to write down the insights. I am often asked to speak at study meetings. I no longer prepare speeches for such occasions, but instead give talks based on the notes I have scribbled down that morning. You can do this kind of practice with a sense of play about it. You can find things lost through oversight, or retrieve memories that have been forgotten. I heartily recommend trying these techniques.

No More Being Late

Let's look at another example. Say you are really busy with your job and have an increasing tendency to be late for appointments. In such a situation, visualize a clock behind your eyelids. Get an inner image of the time you have to arrive at your destination. Let's suppose you have a conference to attend. You visualize yourself having arrived there in time and taking part in it. Beforehand it may look like you are just not going to make it in time, but in fact you do. Or when you have to change trains, visualize arriving at the transfer station with the next train waiting there for you, or just as you arrive at the platform, the next train zooms in with perfect timing. With cars and buses, you can visualize clear passage to avoid red lights or traffic jams. So try this out: Use the inner imagery of adjusting your timing to produce an effect in the real world.

Practicing Quantum Speed-Reading at Bookstores

For adults, for whom left-brain activity is the main focus, the amount of time that can be spent doing QSR training in any 24-hour period is minimal. This makes it difficult to develop the right brain. It is therefore important to begin using the inner imagery in the patterns of daily life. For example, there is a method for changing the way you read books and magazines. First, you just look at the cover and try to imagine what the contents are. Then you flip through the pages to access the information. Next you check the subject matter on the contents page to confirm the results.

Even if you know the books in the new titles section of the bookstore, go ahead and try QSR on them. Since you can do this in a fraction of the time it takes to read them, you may be able quickly to grasp prevalent social trends. With books in familiar genres, there is a tendency for the left brain to interfere, so it is advisable to speed-read books from other fields. By doing that, your way of looking at things will increasingly be altered.

Let's Make Changes in Daily Life

The greater part of our lives has been spent living through the left brain. For that reason, even a stroll down the street unconsciously elicits a left-brain way of walking. It may therefore be a good idea to change your route to work or to school, or even try getting up at a different time. When going to bed, say "Thank you" to your body, expressing your gratitude for all it does for you. When you repeat this again and again, changes start to occur in your body. This may be difficult to grasp logically, but give it a try and see the results. First and foremost, it is important that you acknowledge yourself regularly. I highly recommend that you continue to do these two practices of changing your daily routines and expressing gratitude to your body.

Increasing the Speed of Tasks

Another important general issue is to become more conscious of speed. It is vital that you perform tasks differently and that you slightly increase the speed of doing them. Walking and vacuuming are just two of the many things in daily life you can carry out faster. The right brain is a much deeper part of you and so it is often held in check by the conscious mind or left brain. For that reason, every time you look at printed text, you inadvertently try to read one word at a time. To counteract that tendency, just flip through the pages as if it were a game. I believe it is a good idea to make a practice of flipping through pages whether we understand the content or not. Though we may not consciously understand it, at the subconscious level we clearly grasp the meaning.

8

What I Want to Communicate through Right-Brain Education

It has been said that 98 percent of American children who lose their tempers were abused as small children. When this same study was done in Japan, however, it showed that 80 percent of the children were overprotected.

Progress in Civilization Is What Closed the Right Brain

Humans are creatures of the natural world. The brain is not simply a computer. Because we live in the world of nature, we react sensitively to the changes in color of that natural environment. There is the Earth, the Sun, and the oceans. In spring, the colors are green, and in autumn, they are the rusty brown of fallen leaves.

In the past, people moved about in nature as part of daily life to a far greater extent than they do in the modern world. They had to hunt and tend to their fields for food. The development of civilization has resulted in our only using part of our bodies. At the same time, we have veered toward left-brain domination. When you consider communication between people in our current age, with tools like telephones and e-mail, it is far less of a struggle compared with the past. Our present technological age is indisputably more convenient, but I believe the price we pay is the loss of abilities we had as creatures in touch with the natural world. Paradoxically, I believe that people in the past had more developed right brains and that there were many more intuitive people. Without such abilities, they would not have been able to live in their world. Perhaps with the development of our societies, the need for these abilities has faded and they have atrophied.

Attempting to Open the Closed Right Brain

While it may be true that the right brain has closed down as we have become centered in the left brain, it is not the case that the right brain has atrophied and almost disappeared. No, the right brain is still there. The fact that it does remain surely signifies that as long as humans are alive it is indeed necessary. The same goes for the diencephalon, which is also still active because it, too, is necessary. To reclaim our way of life as creatures of the natural world, both should be put into active use once more. QSR is not a special ability but rather an inherent skill that everybody has and should develop. If we reclaim this skill, a positive shift will occur in our health, our social relationships, our sports endeavors, and other areas.

First, We Must Return Children to Their Natural State

There are all types of children in our society. While many children are flourishing, there are others that seem closed down. What we adults must never forget is that such a situation is often the result of their upbringing. Whereas I feel most comfortable with children who are pure and unrestricted, I certainly encounter others. Some time ago a five-year-old boy came into my classroom with a strange facial tension. Considering that he was only five and should be unblemished, I wondered what was happening in his life to create such tension. The first thing that needs to be done in these cases is to remove the tension from around the eyes. I am not implying that this is always to be done before lessons, but at some point it is important to bring back the "original child" through emotional warmth to relieve the eye stress. Without this step to regain a child's lost vitality, there is no use in doing right-brain exercises.

The Importance of Accepting Existence

On another occasion, there was a girl who came to class with the lock to her inner heart firmly shut. Though she was only a first-grader in elementary school, she must have had a really bad experience or suffered great loneliness. She didn't speak, and whenever I tried to touch her, she would push me aside, making it impossible to work with her. She even said, "I want to quit this Shichida School!"

I thought that rather than forcibly attempting to develop her right-brain skills after such a long period of having her heart closed, it would be better to open the lock gradually. First, I had to accept everything about her and deal with her kindly before commencing with any lessons. This continued for a long time. Two years later, that child finally opened up her heart so fearfully locked. Then she regained her essential qualities as a child. She became able to express herself and was full of life with a smile on her face. At that point, something amazing happened. This stressed-out child, who had locked herself up inside and was unable to do right-brain training, started to flourish as soon as her heart was opened and began to develop new abilities. I have found that even when the children are undergoing painful suffering, they do the lessons properly.

Recognizing Children's Individuality

In QSR, it is important, even before any considerations about whether abilities can be developed, to sit squarely face to face with each child. The prerequisite condition for training is coexistence with and clear recognition of the child. As teachers sit face to face with individual children, they will recognize that there are all different kinds of children. For example, there are children who are like geniuses and very free-thinking, and sometimes they behave in ways that are beyond the understanding of adults. At such times, adults attempt to put them into molds. They tell the child what he or she has to be like, or that at such and such a time he or she has to do the task as told. In many cases, this has the opposite effect. When you try to fit genius children into a mold, they do not become "normal" children and there is a danger of them becoming delinquent. Those who are called geniuses, as in the case of Einstein, need to be raised with the love and support of their parents and teachers.

There are also children who are as sweet as angels. Such children appear to serve the role of pacifiers of the human heart in any single community. It is so important to foster such tender hearts. There are many children, however, who are suffering from stress, as in the previous example of the tense-eyed child. With them, there should be no thought of quickly developing their abilities, but rather of destressing them by starting from the point of accepting them.

So, as we have seen, there are many different types of children in society. We begin by recognizing that they are all unique personalities. Sitting squarely face to face with them is vital. This is the starting point, in my opinion.

If Mothers Are Having Fun, Then So Are the Children

We spend our daily lives in left-brain ways of thinking. In order to utilize the completely different right brain in daily life, we have to move from the world of words to the realm of images. This is not a case of getting it right, but rather a question of getting the feel of it. I believe that if we adults begin to think in this way, then the number of children with stressful expressions in their eyes or who have locked up their hearts will decrease dramatically. In our future education, the way that adults interact with children is going to be crucial. It should not involve stress for the mothers, however, because if they become stressful then they will pass that stress on to their children. It is thus very important for mothers to have fun in their daily lives, to create the right conditions for their child's development.

The Family Meeting around the Hearth Is the Foundation

Professor Toshiyuki Sawaguchi of Hokkaido University has an extremely thought-provoking theory, which is that the Mongoloid race of East Asia has an undeveloped frontal lobe association area at birth. Bcause this area is underdeveloped, infant education becomes crucial. When considering this situation, we realize the great significance of the practice in the past of the grandfather holding counsel with his grandchildren around the hearth. What is absolutely vital for Mongoloid children is to communicate with them through a sensitive love vibration. This shows them how to love in return, so that they can relate to other people, take care of surrounding nature, and not be wasteful with food. This is the basic ingredient for a human being to prosper. In modern society, however, it is often lacking.

In the past, parents and children also did household chores together in order to live. For example, in Japan, when the mother would make miso soup, it was a common everyday scene to see the children preparing the dried fish flakes to put in it. Today it is rare for all the members of a family to sit down and eat together at the dining table. The father returns home late from work, and the children's hours are irregular as they attend cram schools in the evening. The family used to congregate in one place and be able to talk over everyday matters. There were lots of chances for parents and children to be together, for nurturing to occur, but, these days, there are fewer occasions when the family gets together, at the dining table or elsewhere.

Communicating Love and Showing Respect

Growing up in this modern environment, we are like the Mongoloid race whose children's bodies grow but whose frontal lobe association areas remain undeveloped. We think that study alone is important and go from one cram school to another, forgetting about the roots that we must grow to be fully developed human beings. Modern parents may not themselves have had experiences of family communication. It is thus very hard for those with no such experience to convey the message to their children. When it comes to eating meals, all that is considered is the nutritional content of the food, with no thought given to the relationships between people at the dinner table. Yet this communal exchange is surely the most important basis on which to build our lives. The question of whether to emphasize the right or the left brain must follow from the establishment of a strong cultural foundation. For modern society, this base must be first and foremost.

By comparison, because those of Anglo-Saxon origin are born with developed frontal lobe association areas, Americans can learn things more abstractly, like through the media. The Mongoloid races, including the Japanese, do not have completed frontal lobe association areas and thus must have things explained to them in a cultural context. In the past, Japanese had in their daily lives generations of adults who would relate to the children with love, and the children in turn would show respect to the adults. In this way, they would learn about love and respect. This would then grow an important root connection between the brain and the heart of the child.

Right-Brain Development Reveals Our Essential Humanity

The development of the right brain and its abilities in children is currently proceeding rapidly. This is happening through training. As we go about our lives, however, it is surely meaningless to mechanically train the right brain. Since ancient times, people have lived by being connected in communities. Without our greater communal awareness, we begin to live according to habit. Parents raise their children just as they were raised by their parents. Generation upon generation, the same patterns are repeated. If this were to go on without any effect from social changes, there would be no problem. The fact is, however, that changes happening in the world affect us and the way we respond to children. As the children make these abilities their own, they must also, as human beings living in the world, be able to ascertain what is essential to them. So when they become adults, they will be capable of contributing to society in the real sense of the word.

I believe that we should make this our ultimate aim. All parents want their children to be, at the very least, better situated, and all children want to be liked by their parents. Given this, it is important that we keep a firm eye on our children's social development and not simply focus on the studying. We need to raise our children with love and make sure they are not suffering from stress. While parents might think that what they are doing is for the sake of their children, they might, in fact, be unconsciously projecting their own issues on them. Their expectations of their children are based on what they themselves could not achieve, and this becomes a source of stress for the children. Surely, it cannot be considered a gesture of love to presume that children are one and the same as their parents, a presumption that leads to vastly overblown expectations of the children.

Real Enjoyment Does Not Come from Competition

Children coming to the Shichida Child Academy who have been taught by parents that "Being the top student is great" or "You have to beat all the others" will from the outset be overly conscious of having to be number one. At the school, we do not treat that drive in children as something bad, but instead acknowledge that the child is indeed number one. As we progress with children, they discover that the real enjoyment is whether what they are doing is fun. Quite naturally, children become less conscious of being number one in class and start to accept each other. Conversations develop in which they acknowledge that some children are good at doing certain tasks and others are good at different ones.

Let's say, for example, that a child has forgotten his eraser. In that situation, someone would merely toss an eraser to the needy one without thinking "I am such a good kid because I lent him my eraser." We see this daily, where the child who has borrowed an eraser says "Thanks" and then tosses the eraser back, with neither child feeling they had borrowed or lent anything. This, I believe, is very significant. Our value system has long been based on an attitude of give and take. In other words, if you are kind to others, then they will, in turn, be kind to you. In our future society, however, I believe this "give and take" thinking will end. In its place, I believe we will have a value system in which things are openly shared in our social groups at all times.

Right-Brain Feelings Can Be Openly Accepted

Here is another example. There was a child in my class, I. M., who unbeknownst to me had been feeling that he was a victim of bullying. During one lesson, we were speed-reading a blank book with the theme being something you are worried about. We often have interesting themes centered on rare insects of the world or personal stories, but it happened that the mother of one of the students was sick so we decided on this subject. I. M. chose the title "My Bullying" and then started flipping through the blank pages of the book. Because there were so many children doing this lesson, it was hard to check the results one by one. At the start, I was not aware of what was happening to I. M. Suddenly, I realized he was hanging his head in total silence. I thought this was strange and asked him what was wrong.

He explained about the bullying and then replied, "I'm going to apologize to my friend tomorrow."

Since it was strange for him to apologize for being the victim, I asked him, "Why apologize?"

His reply was, "I thought that I hated him for bullying me but realized I had said something really nasty to him before it all started."

In other words, I. M. was to blame in the matter. This led him to the decision to apologize the next day and say, "It was my fault."

Because falling-outs are emotional problems, though we may understand them logically, it is hard for us to humble ourselves in dealing with them. In doing QSR, however, we are not simply looking at images to understand things, but dealing with right-brain perceptions.

Deep emotions and feelings of consideration for others tend to ooze out of our perceptional pores. Such profound sentiments are then able to be humbly accepted. It goes without saying that the bullying problem of this particular child ended on that day.

In QSR, we normally focus on the book images or colors that emerge. But after having done this for many years, it became obvious that the children's facial expressions were becoming brighter and brighter in the process. I can only conclude that there must be some stimulation, at the most intrinsic levels, of the children's consciousness.

Discipline through the Five Senses

As we have seen thus far, the changing times have weakened family bonds greatly, and the discipline required to raise children properly is now insufficient for the job. Yet it may be hard to argue that this is only due to the times in which we live. Even in the past, it was by no means the case that father would come straight home from work and have dinner with the children. Just as in this modern age, there were jobs where workers came home late and left very early in the morning, but proper discipline existed. It is therefore not vital that parents always be present to discipline their children properly. As an example, even if the father is not at the dinner table, his position could be designated with his rice bowl and chopsticks in place to create a sense of his presence. Or in a household in which the father returns home after the children have gone to sleep, if his pajamas are left in the laundry basket for the children to see them the next morning, his presence will again be felt.

We might say that this is raising children through the sense of sight. In other words, the parents do not necessarily have to be there at the children's side at all times; a parent's discipline can be reinforced a great deal visually, or with the other senses. When children come home in the evening and say, "I'm back!" but don't see their mother standing in the kitchen, they can feel her presence in the smell of curried rice cooking for dinner or the great smell of chestnuts. It is not through words alone that we discipline them. It is necessary for us to raise them as whole human beings at the most fundamental level across the entire range of daily life.

If It's Fun for Children, They Will Do It

If the environment is conducive and the children are relieved of stress, they are able to enjoy anything and everything. This includes the lessons that are part of right-brain training. At the beginning, it might be fun being number one in the class when part of a competitive system, but sooner or later they will get bored with it. If we really want our children to lead full lives, I think we need to realize that if it's fun for children, they will do it.

Another crucial point is that a good university or job posting should not become the sole focus of attention. We are no longer in an age where name value has any meaning. What is more important than forcing such status on children is that they be raised with a rich sensitivity to help them discover their own direction. This will activate the children's minds to find the profession they most want to pursue, and even if they fail, they will be able to climb out of it. If they are always moving along the tracks laid down by their parents, whatever happens, they will ask their parents what they should do next. What kind of school should I go to next, or what should I do now, or where should I get a job, and so on. With that kind of dependency, it is impossible to stand on your own two feet. Moreover, when the children experience failure, they won't take responsibility, but will say instead, "It's because you told me to do it." The aim of child-rearing should be to make children independent. We should never lose sight of this independence, on the part of both the parent and the child. Let's consider how best to accomplish that from here on.

Let's Inspire Confidence in Children

Here are some affirmations for daily life that I wish to mention. Foremost is: "It is truly wonderful that you have been born as a human being." From the point of view of our brain structure, there is a mere 0.05 percent difference between the abilities of a genius and those of a normal person. This suggests that there is amazing ability within each of us. There is no need for us to try to be like other people. Doing things our own way is fine. From that point, our unique personality emerges. If we consider the multifaceted structure of our minds, all of the answers lie within us. By using this suggestion and believing in our own sensibility, we will be able to move forward in life. In the current social atmosphere, there are a lot of people with ability who lack confidence in themselves and are incapable of standing on their own two feet. Without independence, we are unable to take responsibility for ourselves and end up blaming others.

It is because I see so many young people in this condition that I want to help them grow up. "The answer lies within you" is what we are stressing here. For example, in answer to the question "Do I like myself?" many people would answer "No!" Not many people can say, "I really like myself a lot." The feeling of really liking oneself is based on a sense of harmony with existence. That comes from nurturing that little child within us. To start, try going back to yourself as a fetus and asking what your mission is and what is the meaning of your being born at this time.

9

Right-Brain Education in the Womb

A child from one family said, "Mum, I remember talking to Dad when I was inside your tummy. I saw him from inside. And I saw two chimneys."

Increasing Amniotic Fluid Acidity Is the Natural Enemy of the Fetus

For fertilization to occur, a single-celled egg is sent down the fallopian tube to the uterus where the 50 million sperm jostle to fertilize it. One sperm succeeds and enters the egg, dies after crashing into the flagellum, and becomes a source of protein. A strange thing occurs when 50 million sperm surge in and around the egg, however. One part of the egg opens up like an entrance. The cause of this is thought to be sound. There is no ear or mouth or head to this egg, yet the surging sound of the sperm opens an entrance. In all probability, this sound is related to the right brain. It might be possible to say that this exchange is a kind of telepathy. In this way, fertilization is constituted. Because it is a single-celled egg, it has sensibility, memory, and its own disposition. Thus the diencephalon of the fetus can be stimulated and positive sensibility, memory, and disposition can be inputted. This is fetal education.

The fetus grows inside amniotic fluid that is like sweet and sour seawater. In this fluid, the fetus sucks its fingers, yawns, and sloshes about. The normal pH of amniotic fluid is about 7.8. But the pH can change. For example, if the mother decides to go shopping and forgets her purse, the ensuing tension is enough to drop the pH to 5 in a couple of seconds. A marital quarrel and its emotional energy are enough to drop the level down to 3 in a flash. These pH level decreases mean that there is more acidity in the amniotic fluid. The baby in the womb is happily sucking on a finger and suddenly the taste becomes sour. The amniotic fluid ceases to be a relaxing environment comfortable to the baby, and so its body stiffens up.

At the same time, the baby hears the sounds of mother's beating heart, the pulsing sound of her blood flowing, her bones squeaking and creaking—all as a kind of background music. However, when the mother gets emotional, her beating heart speeds up, as does her blood circulation. The creaking of the bones gets harsher. Amidst this noise pollution and acidic amniotic fluid is no place for a mind to develop. It is for this reason that fetal education is so important.

Speaking to Babies in the Womb

The main objective of fetal education is for mothers to communicate love to the babies in their wombs. With right-brain sensibility, it is possible to "talk" in this way. For example, when there are 20 babies present and only one of them has been involved in a proper fetal education, I am able to pick that one out right away. That is how great the effect of intrauterine education can be. Children thus born are good-natured and not shy of strangers. They are bright and have a sense of presence about them. Mothers coming to the Shichida Child Academy who have done fetal educational training get through their birthing quickly. In some fast cases, it only takes 15 minutes. Because the babies so educated can sense, using their diencephalon, it is important to communicate a variety of messages to the baby in the womb. One can be to throw disease-bearing pathogens into the amniotic fluid before they are born.

By sensing with the diencephalon, I mean it is possible to have telepathic conversations. An example is to ask the baby in the womb to tell you when its father is coming home and to signal it by kicking. If it gets quiet after such kicking, it means the baby has gone to sleep. In a situation like that, the mother could say, "I'm sorry! There's no need to inform me when you are sleeping" and thus gain a further level of communication. Another example is when the mother is on the phone and feels a tap, tap inside. She then asks the baby, "Did you want to talk on the phone?" To which the baby quips back, "Yes, I did," and tells the mother its message. So we can see that right-brain communication can even occur with babies in the womb. At the same time, since the baby is floating in an amniotic sea of its mother's love, an even deeper bond is forged.

Seeing Scenery from inside the Womb

We have seen that mothers can communicate with their babies through fetal education. What about the fathers? The mothers are physically connected to the babies, but that is not the case with the fathers. That being said, the fathers can also communicate with the babies in the womb. One example is for the father to face the mother's belly in the morning and say, "I'm off to the office now!" That alone is enough to establish communication with the baby. In the evenings, children tend to generate alpha brain waves and start to get sleepy. It was at such a time that a child from one family said, "Mum, I remember talking to Dad when I was inside your tummy. I saw him from inside. And I saw two chimneys." Because the family had moved just before this child was born, there was no way he could have seen the chimneys after birth. From the apartment where the family lived while he was in the womb, two chimneys could indeed be seen. When his mother asked how he knew about those chimneys, he replied, "Because I saw them from inside your tummy!" Amazing occurrences like this are common.

The Child Picks the Parents

When the parent-child relationship becomes stormy, we have to begin child care all over again by going back to the womb. I sometimes hear children say, "There's no way I should have been born to parents like this," but that is an absurd statement to make. In such cases, we must take the child to a level where they will understand that they picked the parents they were born to. And if we then ask our child, "You chose me for a mother, didn't you?" they will invariably nod yes. This will surely encourage her to raise the child with real love since she has been chosen. The mother can say to the child, "Thank you so much for choosing me as your mother."

Child-Rearing without Discrimination but with Proper Choices

Fetal education is not limited to the positive relationships that develop between the parents and the fetus. Let's say that a child is born who quickly understands that "I have got really affectionate parents." Perhaps the grandparents are also around and there is an older brother in the picture as well. Until now, the parents have focused all their attention on this first child, but now everybody's eyes are on the new baby! For this reason, the first child tends to have feelings of loneliness. He might then say to his parents, "Mum and Dad, you are always cuddling the baby, and maybe he's cute but I don't want him around!" In child-rearing, we must not discriminate between our children but rather make proper choices with them. We have first to give our love to the child who is feeling left out and lonely. For the second child born into a family, it is totally normal for him to have a sibling and to have to share the parents' love, but for the first child, this sharing requires adjustment.

The Importance of "Skinship"

Generally, what happens is that suddenly one day a new child is born and we lose track of the children already here. When there is a three-year gap between the children, it is not as much of a problem as it is when the ages are closer together. In the latter situation, the first child can experience loneliness. It is vital for us first to take care of this child's needs. Of course, the most important focus of love should be the amniotic fluid where new life grows, but love needs to be expressed to the older child in that environment very close to the amniotic fluid, which is the bathtub. There we must soap the child's body just as a mother cat would lick her kitten's body to clean it. Then please show your gratitude there by saying, "Thank you. Because you have been so good, our baby is growing up properly. Will you please be good from now on?"

In making the child responsible, your affection and respect will sink in deeply, and the older child's feelings will change to, "OK! I'll take care of the little baby then!" In this way, not only does the parent-child relationship improve, but so too does the sibling one. This is not limited to the bathtub, but can be in reading picture books together in bed. This, too, is a good way to communicate our love to the older child. By doing such things, the child can reclaim feelings of being loved and get his or her bouncing energy back.

Both adults and children have gestures that serve as signs for how they are feeling. For example, a child sucking its thumb or a dejected facial expression can tell us that something is wrong. In raising children, it is a good idea to read their gestures. If we are unaware of these gestures and their emotional cues, this will lead to them acting them out by bumping into furniture or dropping a cup of milk. Before that happens, we should nip it in the bud by realizing what the gestures are showing us and dealing with it.

Skillful Parents Rear Children by Making Everything Enjoyable

As noted previously, parents tend to raise their children the way they themselves were raised. If the patterns transmitted down through the generations are wholesome, then no matter how the times change the children will be raised properly. Traditionally, when giving toys to a baby or young child, a skillful mother will first play with the toy herself and invite the child to play by saying, "Look how much fun it is to play with this!" As the child intently looks, his hesitant little hand reaches out to begin playing with it. This way is more fun for the child, too. If there is something difficult involved for the little one, the mother lends a hand and says, "Here's how you do it!" The result will be that the baby is soon able to play with the toy by himself. In this process, both the mother and the child have fun.

This approach need not be taught to some mothers—they already use it—whereas others cannot put it into practice even when taught. (If their parents didn't teach them this way, they may have a hard time teaching it, in turn.) Children who have been raised in this enjoyable manner tend to have a rich sensibility. Whenever such a child says something, we feel instinctively drawn in by him or her. It is my feeling that children like this have an atmosphere about them (a vibration or a field effect) that makes us want to resonate in tune with them.

Growing the Child's Sense of Being in the First Three Months

For the first three months after birth, the prime focus should be on raising the child to have a sense of being. Through hugging them, we communicate our love with a basic animal instinct just as cats lick kittens. Because we humans are creatures of the natural world, we need to have animal expressions of love during the first three months. This allows the baby to develop a sense of being, by which I mean that the baby recognizes its own existence. Even though the baby is still small, it gets a clear sense of itself as a person and can start to live a subjective life.

Perseverance and Optimism

At the age of four months when the baby starts to cry, before picking up the baby, the parent should wait ten seconds after asking, "What are you crying about?" This will develop some perseverance in the baby. The next step is at eight months. At this stage, some kind of exciting movement is required. If this is done too early, the brain, which is still undeveloped inside the skull, may suffer some damage. At about eight months, the child is ready and it is Dad's turn to make an entrance. This is when Dad will lift the baby up in the air again and again, eliciting chuckles of delight. Through such exciting movement, the baby will have positive feelings, grow actively, and be full of life. On the other hand, babies who do not play in this way tend to give in to fear and be pessimistic as they grow up.

The Soul of a Three-Year-Old Lasts to a Hundred

The next stage is at a year and a half. This is where the baby starts to express himself clearly. In our class for mothers, I often hear the comment, "You were such a good baby, I wonder where I went wrong?" This stage is really a sign of growth, however. We should actually welcome this development and, rather than putting a lid on it, warmly observe its growth. Then we get to the very crucial ages of two and three years. Because the child has by now developed an ego and is frustrated by limitations, he will throw himself down and start crying in his frustration. For example, at times when he wants to play with a new toy, his mother will tell him to put it away. Since the child has not yet acquired the left-brain intellectualization to understand why, he will start crying to get his way. It is a transitory phase of the child's growth process. By the age of four or five, this will stop as if a storm has blown over.

Children grow up through this process, much like a caterpillar becomes a butterfly, and so it is vital that we grasp the importance of this experience for the child. Crying and screaming are simply transitory stages. By the age of three, the foundations of a human being have been built. These three aspects of growth—the transformation, the crying, and the foundation—have to be fully accepted by parents who are able to deal with the great variety of changes they entail. Then the stages of child-rearing that follow will be much easier. There is a proverb that says, "The soul of a three-year-old lasts to a hundred," and that means that the period from the womb through the age of three represents the most important time in raising a child.

We humans are animals. We need to grow up as biological beings that are also gifted with reason. That is why we cannot raise children simply with reason, but must also incorporate an animal type of instinctual love.

Being Born Again by Returning to the Womb

Almost all mothers have concerns about their children when the latter are around six years old. By that age, children enrolled at Shichida Child Academy have already gone through the most crucial period in their infant education. It is therefore a little late to be told something that should have been taken care of by the pivotal age of three. This is one of the strong points of the Shichida style of education, however. Using mental imagery, we can take the mother back to her pregnancy, when the child was in her womb, and go through it again.

Let's give an example. One mother who attended Mr. Shichida's lecture had two children, a fifth-grader and a baby. The eldest son was troublesome. It seemed that nothing could be done about his poor schoolwork and so she felt resigned to the situation.

She decided, however, that things would be different with the younger child, and she gathered information on various educational theories. At this point, I shared the idea with the mother that the "problem" child was merely a reflection of herself. When I told her that the child had no responsibility in the manner in which she had raised him, tears began welling up in her eyes. This particular mother now realized that the fault lay with her and not her son, and she was deeply remorseful about it. She revealed to me that she had not wanted to have that child, but had gone ahead anyway. She had raised the child without giving much love to him. I then suggested to her that she apologize for that and then use mental imagery to return to the time when he was still in the womb and to lavish him with feelings of love and acceptance.

For the first lesson, we had the mother mentally stand in front of the child and say, "Let's go through your birth again," and then imagine putting the child back into the womb. After that, she relived the whole pregnancy, stage by stage, but this time communicating love to the fetus. As the final stage of the birth approached in this imaging, she said to the fetus, "Drop all the bad feelings in the womb and have an easy birth." The baby was then born all over again, and the image this time was that of a delighted mother and father.

At the next lesson, with both mother and child present, there was a situation in which the child could not get something done. The mother would normally have scolded him at this point, but on that day she apologized to him from her heart. Tears welled up in the child's eyes as he looked straight at his mother. This was a child who, before, never cried. But due to his mother's apology, something inside him opened up. Feeling the effect of his mother's mental imagery, being back in the womb and then being reborn, a new ability began to flower within him like a cherry blossom opening. It was as though a hard bud had suddenly burst open due to the spring breeze blowing over it.

In due course, as everything harmonized, this boy developed ESP abilities. He was able to see through cards. If he had grown up as he was, he might have been a social outcast all his life. But a new birth takes place from the moment of realization. Anything and everything can be reset. Please remember this point: It is always possible to relive the past and make it right.

It's Never Too Late to Foster the Power of Children

There is no need to take a pessimistic view if the raising of your child is not going well. At times, you may not even like yourself, but this is by no means a reason to feel depressed. Raising children is not just about bringing up a child. What about the little child inside you? It is never too late—no matter what your age—to nurture yourself. It could be that you did not receive enough love in childhood and are carrying emotional wounds, and for that reason never seem to get on well in life. Are you one of those people who, for the sake of their job, children, spouse, or parents, end up never doing what they want for themselves, even though there are many things they want to do in life? Although right-brain education to open neural pathways is best completed by the age of ten, it is by no means too late to start as an adult. In fact, if people with nothing but left-brain training begin to practice right-brain learning, there will be a balance of both, which in itself opens up the diencephalon. So it is not too late to start.

Please go ahead and tackle the development of your right brain. Remember that when people start to develop new abilities such as ESP, it tends to entrance them. Please do not forget that right-brain development is best utilized by a balance with the left brain, and that both are required for love and harmony to be present. Without a mind-set of love and harmony, the diencephalon will not become developed. We could say then that those people who develop the right brain have hearts and minds full of love and harmony. I believe that if there were increasing numbers of people with highly developed right-brain talents in balance with the left brain (which opens the diencephalon), there would eventually be no more war. I cannot help but hope that many people are encouraged to take right-brain training, opening the doors of the diencephalon and living lives brimming with love.

10

Practice Program

So let's do Quantum Speed-Reading. To review, the way QSR works is that flipping through the pages of a book at high speed switches on the right-brain computer. What makes QSR different from general speed-reading is that a book is "bounced through" in a flash. In this way, the quantum vibrations emanating from the book are transformed into light and imagery—the information by which the contents of the book can be understood. The following are the right-brain functions activated in QSR:

• The right brain's autotranslation function: Foreign languages change to the reader's language.

• The right brain's imaging function: Words change to images.

• The right brain's script-changing function: For Japanese readers, kanji characters change to phonetic hiragana script.

The Benefits of QSR

Fast reading is only the beginning of the benefits of QSR. Through doing QSR, positive changes occur in the following areas of life:

- Speed and processing ability
- Personal relations, including the parent-child relationship
- Work
- Study
- Health
- Development of talents
- Art
- Sports

Program for Infants and Toddlers

0–2 Years
- Mother speaking to the child

- Daily life experiences

- Reading picture books with child (i.e., picture book with a few words and big letters, frequently repeated, with the child speaking when old enough)

2–4 Years
Basic Point: Communicating mother's love fully through skinship, that is, cuddling, hugging, and bathing

- Imaginary stories in which the child is the hero

- Playing at being something or somebody

- Playing with toy dishes with Mom in the kitchen

- Playing outside in nature

- Playing with friends

- Picture books (i.e., eight-page picture book); rereading books to the child that he or she enjoys

4–6 Years
- Child speaking with friends

- Playing in groups (e.g., at preschool)

- Picture books and other books (i.e., widening the scope to include books adults enjoy, too)

- QSR: (1) Flying in to your mom's belly (the womb), in to your own body, and in to books; (2) Mother shows how to flip through books (without checking the contents)

Program for Children (Elementary Grades)

Step 1: Basic staring practice, afterimage training with the orange card and campfire, 3D stereograms, and eye training.

Step 2: Image training with breathing techniques, sounds of the ocean; balloons; flying in to your own body, in to fruits, and in to books.

Step 3: Quantum Speed-Reading. Begins with relaxation, then concentration, visualizing lying on the back, then three deep breaths, the rod imaging, the artificial light training, flying in to a book, flying in to a specific page of the book, checking the content by verbalizing it and writing it down as words and pictures.

Step 4: Quantum Speed-Reading. Staring practice, afterimage training, eye training, lying down and breathing deeply, rod imaging, artificial light training, blindfolded QSR, QSR with colors from a book, images and messages from the book, and book content (what the author was feeling, your own thoughts on it).

Program for Adults

Step 1: Breathing exercises, afterimage training with the orange card and campfire, solar glimpsing, 3D stereograms, and eye training ("camera shutter" training); total time required about 10–20 minutes.

Step 2: Image training in colors, with the seven rainbow colors and red, yellow, and green; the front door exercise; flying in to your own body, in to fruits, and in to books.

Step 3: Quantum Speed-Reading. Begins with relaxation, then concentration, visualizing lying on the back, then three deep abdominal breaths (mental training), rod imaging, artificial light training, flying in to a book, flying in to specific pages of the book, checking the content by verbalizing it and writing it as words and pictures.

Step 4: Quantum Speed-Reading. Staring practice, afterimage training, eye training, lying down and doing abdominal breathing three times (mental training), rod imaging, artificial light training, blindfolded QSR, QSR with colors from the book, images and messages from the book, book content (what the author was feeling, your own thoughts and feelings on it).

How to Proceed through Steps 1 to 4
Step 1: Basic Training

Staring Practice: Flowers

First of all, let's relax by taking longer and deeper breaths and releasing mental and physical stress. Look at the word below as you regulate your breathing. Try to blink as little as possible and keep on staring. You will start to see images (if you don't, it's fine just to think about it). Changing words into images leads to being able to speed-read books and then see images emitted from them related to the content.

FLOWER

As you breathe in, the word appears to float closer; as you breathe out, it gets farther away. What kind of imagery do you see? What kinds of flowers are appearing? Write down their names.

Staring Practice: The Campfire

Stare at the campfire picture (see color section), blinking as little as possible. This is the basic training that will empower your image visualization.

Stare at the black dot in the middle of the green fire for 30 seconds. Next stare at the lower black dot. You will then see a red fire dimly above the logs (if you continue to stare, it will gradually appear). If you see nothing, then breathe quietly and slowly and start over. By continuing to practice, you'll be able to see the afterimage for longer durations.

Staring Practice: The Orange Card

Breathe deeply three times, relax your mind, and stare at the blue circle (see color section) for 30 seconds. Close your eyes and you will see the afterimage. If it disappears while you are practicing, think to yourself, "It will reappear," and it will do so.

The four stages to being able to visualize images are:

1. In the beginning, you will see a secondary color, orange.

2. Then you will see the same color afterimage in blue.

3. The color and the shape of the afterimage can then be changed (e.g., a red circle, a green square).

4. After that, you will spontaneously be able to see images.

You will deepen your image-making ability by repeating the exercise over and over.

Solar Glimpse Training

The pituitary gland in the diencephalon is activated by doing this exercise. First thing in the morning (before 9:00, if possible), gaze at the sun directly for a second. Close your eyes and practice looking at the afterimage. Even on rainy days, you can do this exercise by visualizing that the sun is out. Your body will get healthier, too.

3D Training

These are three-dimensional staring practices.

Pansies (3D): This is a practice to be able to see the unseen. The right brain is activated by the way the eyes are used here. Do not focus on the pansies (see color section). You will see two dots at the bottom become three and, at that point, the stereographic image will appear on the page.

The mandalas: They will be merged together. Use an open gaze to see beyond (behind) the picture (see color section) by not focusing the eyes. In this way, you will see the two mandalas become one. Practicing this exercise will awaken a new sensation in you.

Eye Training

Basic training: Move eyes up and down, then left and right, and then diagonally.

Further applications: Move eyes in a star shape.

- Eye training improves eyeball movement, widens the field of vision, and heightens the ability to read at a glance.

- Ten seconds should be spent on each exercise.

- Do not move the head, just the eyes. Correct posture and breathing are important in this exercise.

- If you can use a metronome or a similar instrument, it will be an effective aid.

Adult Practice in "Camera Shutter" Eye Training

This is done by rapid blinking so the brain will not know if the eyes are open or closed. It is vital to increase the speed of blinking

Four Eye Training Exercises
(practicing to widen the field of vision)

1. Up/down movement

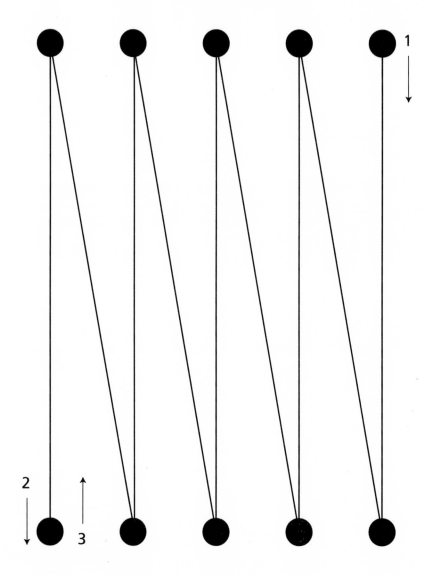

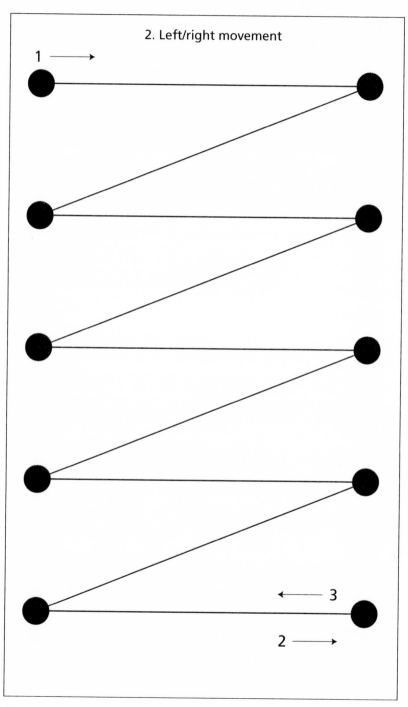

3. Up/down diagonal (Part 1)

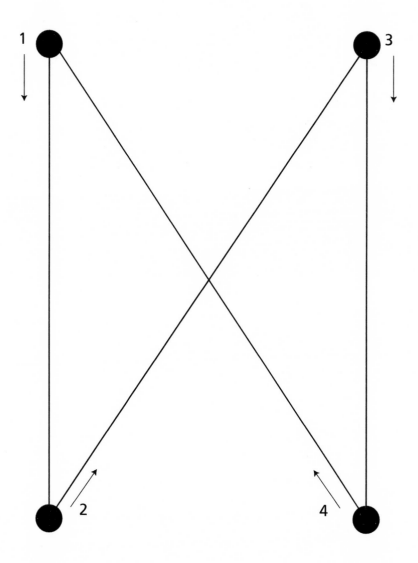

4. Up/down diagonal (Part 2)

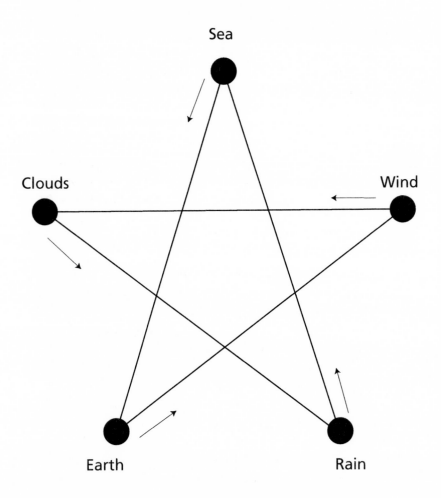

(The order goes: wind, clouds, rain, sea, earth.)

to your utmost ability. In doing so, you will be able to see light and colors. These exercises are aimed at increasing the visual field acuity. Please refer to the specified picture for each (you can make enlarged copies of the picture, if you prefer):

- Eye Training 1 (p. 87): Up/down movement
- Eye Training 2 (p. 88): Left/right movement
- Eye Training 3 (p. 89): Up/down diagonal (part 1)
- Eye Training 4 (p. 90): Up/down diagonal (part 2). The order goes: wind, clouds, rain, sea, and earth in the five-pointed star.

Step 2: Image Training with Breath Regulation
Sea Waves
Take deep, long breaths, exhaling through the mouth. Now imagine you are standing on a sandy beach. The waves are lapping in and out. Match your breathing to the rhythm of the waves. As the wave comes in, breathe in. As the waves go out, so does your breath. Take long, deep breaths, exhaling through pursed lips.

The Balloon
Imagine you are standing on a vast plain. A balloon, swaying in the wind, comes into sight. As you breathe in, the balloon sways closer; as you breathe out, it moves farther away. Breathe deeply as you visualize this swaying balloon.

Flying In
In this exercise, you become microscopic and go deeper and deeper into something. Close your eyes. Behind your eyelids, you can see a huge mirror. You are standing in front of it. You become half of your reflected size, and then half of that again and again until your body has become an invisible particle.

- Fly in to your body. This is an exploration of the inside of your body. You can quickly move there. Is it healthy or not in there? Ask the cells what they want you to do, and then go and do it for them.

• Fly in to a fruit. Check the seeds. How many can you spot? Where did you see them? Write this information down on a piece of paper. After you have done the flying-in exercise, cut open the fruit and check your results.

• Fly in to a book. Go inside a book and see what is written there and what pictures it contains.

Image Training for Adults

The key to developing imaging power is in the breath.

1. Out breath (imagine toxic energy in your body leaving)—5 seconds

2. In breath (energy from the universe comes into your body)—5 seconds

3. Between breaths (inhaled energy is pushed down into the lower abdomen)—5 seconds

You can make these steps last longer as you get used to the exercise.

Rainbow Colors. Look at colors (see color section) in the progression red, orange, yellow, green, blue, indigo, and violet. Look at the surrounding visual field. Close your eyes and visualize the colors, beginning with red and then one after another. Visualize the whole field of color.

Red, Blue, Green, the House Entrance. You can also practice the afterimage training with the orange card. Visualize red apple, yellow banana, green watermelon, and then you see your own front door. Open the door. Is there anybody standing inside? Go through the whole house and see what is happening there. Note that you must check your results after finishing.

(For elementary school children, an adult should read the sentences out loud to them. For adults, after reading the sentence, you can move into the world of imagery.)

Step 3

It's time at last for Quantum Speed-Reading. There are a few exercises to do, however, before we get to flipping book pages.

Relaxation (for adults)

Move your body around and de-stress yourself; you might do abdominal crunches, a headstand, push-ups, or the back-bridge exercise.

Mental Training (for adults)

Do abdominal breathing first, then see yourself in a positive light and as one who can access your highest power.

Rod (Stick) Imaging

Lie quietly on the floor. Close your eyes and take three deep breaths at your own pace. As you breathe in, visualize yourself as a hard rod, counting one, two, and three as you stiffen. Lift your back up from the floor a couple of inches and hold for about 10 seconds. As you release your out breath, you return to the floor and become supple and soft. Repeat the stiffening and release three times each.

Artificial Light Training

For this exercise, you need a lamp stand with a naked 30-watt light bulb; fluorescent tubes will not work. (You can omit this exercise if you do not have a standard lamp.) Gaze at the light bulb from a distance of 6.5 feet for about 30 seconds without blinking. Then switch off the light, close your eyes, and observe the afterimage.

Quantum Speed-Reading (flying in to books)

Hold a wrapped book in both hands, say to yourself, "This book is a friend," and imagine yourself becoming one with the book. Concentrate and then fly in to the book. Write or draw the contents of what you saw or felt in the book. (An important point: A picture book is recommended at the beginning.)

Quantum Speed-Reading (flying in to specific pages of the book)

In this exercise, you fly in to specific pages in a book, decided on beforehand. Details of how to proceed can be found in the last section of chapter 5 (page 49).

Step 4: QSR

Flipping the pages of a book

See step 3 for the recommended start-off method. After doing the rod imaging, visualize the following:

• See yourself flipping through the pages.
• See colors being emitted by the book.
• See yourself understanding the contents.

Blindfold QSR

You can either make it too dark to see the book or put on a blindfold. Hold the book in both hands and, as you concentrate, imagine that you and the book are becoming one.

Flip through the pages, getting faster and then slower by turn. What colors, images, or messages are you receiving? Flip through the pages holding the book above your head, next to your ear, in front of your nose, in front of your chest, and in other positions.

QSR

Take off the blindfold and do QSR while actually looking at the book. Flip through the book pages, now faster, now slower. See if you can grasp the colors, the images, and the content.

Note 1: Books to Be Read by QSR. Begin with books that you have already read. Get the feel of what it is like to do QSR of a book whose contents you have already grasped.

Basic points to look for: A book that has a clear argument, contents related to nature, or is, in short, a good book.

Further development: As you get better, move on to business books or textbooks, and others that might interest you.

Note 2: Images Coming from the Book (for Adults). Anybody can sense the colors and messages coming from books. Although some people are naturals at this process, it might be necessary for others to participate in a seminar to sense the imagery emitted from the books. The reason for doing so is that it is important to be able to observe the images clearly.

In repeating this training over and over, there will come a time when suddenly you know, "This is what it feels like to be doing it." Therefore, please carry on practicing!

Review

Here follows a quote by Dr. Sawaguchi from his book *The Brain and Infant Education,* published by Bungei Shinsho: "We learn a lot of life's wisdom from the sandpit at the kindergarten preschool. Then on the plains of life we learn the necessary bases to be a scientist. I feel that what I learned at the peak of that mountain that is graduate school was just specialized knowledge and technical skills."

The Infant Training Program

The foundation of "Child Power" lies in a child's infancy. I think children who have been raised in the abundant love of their mothers will use this ability for love and for peace. In due course, they will return to their mothers' sides.

In natural surroundings, where the children are playing together, they are full of loving feelings. Playing games that connect them to their mothers and sitting on their mothers' laps reading a picture book are experiences that form the foundation for amazing abilities. In these ways, children's minds and bodies are educated.

The Children's Program

In terms of the methodology of how to teach elementary students, please use a blend of both right- and left-brain techniques for learning.

1. When arranging timetables at school, use the time until the teacher comes to class, after the bell has sounded, to practice doing QSR.

2. Quite apart from QSR, children should read storybooks and have fun by putting themselves in the position of the hero as they read.

3. Do QSR on all genres of books as well as different languages. It makes no difference how easy or difficult the books are.

4. For those taking exams, please keep track of results over time. The following points are important:

- Flip the pages of schoolbooks.

- Check the colors emitted from the books and the language changes.

- Use red-orange-yellow detection, then on to green-blue-purple (right-brain practice).

- What is the message from the book saying about the method of study? How should the learning process be done?

The Adult Program

Do the training as a way of reading a book so that, after you have finished, you find yourself flipping through the pages of any book that comes into your hands. Please allow books to naturally become part of your daily life.

- Before you begin training, take the Child Power Test. Afterward, take it again.

- Please just single-mindedly continue to repeat the exercises.

- What is blindfolded QSR? To see objects within your visual field of perception is a wonderful ability, but we tend to become overwhelmed by the printed words in books. The reason is that our surface consciousness alone is operating. When the student is blindfolded, the surface consciousness is interrupted and the deeper levels of consciousness get activated. The book's contents are then fully grasped. This deeper level of consciousness is very important.

- QSR is a speed-reading technique that awakens the diencephalon. Being able to do QSR means that you have the ability to image things. That is what we call "Child Power." Take the Child Power Test again and again, to track the changes. QSR activates the essential aspect of our consciousness (diencephalon). As a result of doing QSR, many wondrous things begin to happen.

The Child Power Test for Adults

Check the boxes that apply to you. Take the test before commencing training, and then again after completion.

Statement	Before Training	After Training
1 I dream in color.	❏	❏
2 I can concentrate at work.	❏	❏
3 Images appear easily.	❏	❏
4 Things that I visualize happening, do happen.	❏	❏
5 I have no anxiety or stress.	❏	❏
6 I have good intuition and get flashes of understanding.	❏	❏
7 I rarely get angry.	❏	❏
8 I can make judgments at work and have little hesitation.	❏	❏
9 I often get feelings of kindness.	❏	❏
10 I get ideas.	❏	❏
11 I have a bright personality.	❏	❏
12 My work conditions are good.	❏	❏
13 I am good at remembering people's names.	❏	❏
14 I am healthy (do not catch colds) and do not get sick or hurt.	❏	❏
15 I don't worry about the past or future. I can focus on the now.	❏	❏
16 My family life runs smoothly.	❏	❏
17 I have good decision-making skills.	❏	❏
18 I read books quickly.	❏	❏

19 I am not often annoyed or upset.   ❏   ❏
20 I smile more often than not.   ❏   ❏
21 I easily connect with the things
    and people I need.   ❏   ❏

Count one point for each box checked.
21 points: You have a great deal of Child Power! You can do QSR.
11–20: Excellent! You have quite a lot of Child Power.
6–10: Average.
Under 5: You have a lot of stress. Get back to being a child and
          relax!

Afterword

Quantum Speed-Reading did not emerge as a technique as a result of adults forcefully teaching it to children. It arose much like a game from the casual and unconscious activities of the children. It is for this reason that we call the innocent and fancy-free principle of QSR "Child Power." What kind of power is this then? When we asked the children how to best help adults to gain the power of imaging, one child replied: "You should just remember more and more what is was like to be kids." Let's remember then what it was like when we were children: swimming in the river until the sun set, the stag beetle we caught with friends, playing at being mothers. We were so free and so innocent at heart. Try flipping through the pages of a book with that sense of anticipation as you reclaim your childhood self. Sense the marvelous power welling up in you. This is where Quantum Speed-Reading begins.

Getting Rid of Stereotypes

Because so much of our daily lives is centered on the left brain, we tend to think that is the only way to live. We are almost unaware of the fact that the right brain has amazing abilities. So if we are to use that ability, we will have to start by breaking the mold of left-brain thinking. In doing this, we will move away from the world of language, theory, and logic, and connect to the world of imagery. It will then become possible for us to glimpse a mysterious and unseen realm. Please do not judge the right-brain world with the left-brain yardstick of what can and cannot be done, or of guessing what is right or wrong. By making free use of the right brain and having it as part of our daily life, we should realize that a new way of life is possible. The most crucially important thing for our future is that our everyday consciousness and our essential consciousness blend into one.

Child Power Awakens the Diencephalon

A simple way of explaining how QSR works in relationship to our brain is that the pineal gland, situated within the diencephalon, acts as a receptor-transmitter base of quantum-level information. The skin serves the function of an overall receiving and transmitting cover on the outside of the human body. Information acquired by the skin is communicated to nerve cells and arrives at the pineal gland in the diencephalon via the right brain. That information is translated into images, which we can then see. When we flip through the pages of a book, information from the eyes and the skin is sent to the brain and becomes images or something we can feel or hear. This is what is meant by opening up the diencephalon. It is not too much perhaps to say that QSR utilizes the entire brain. And this QSR ability should not be understood as something particularly occult. When you consider the structure and the functioning of the brain, these abilities are simply an extension of already existing powers. Even if you can't visualize any imagery, just keep practicing it and get used to it as you would brushing your teeth every day. By continuing to practice, you will be connected to a deeper level of consciousness.

QSR Is Just the Beginning

Maybe some people will think, "Why don't we just read books the normal way instead of doing this QSR?" It is, of course, important in QSR to comprehend the contents of a book, but this is really just the beginning. Changes start to occur in our daily lives, in the areas of our health, study, and work. We discover another way of living that is different from what we have known so far. This is where the greatest objective lies.

QSR Is for Everybody

In this book, I have talked about child-rearing, elementary school children's training, students undergoing exam preparation, and specific techniques for adults. Please refer to the relevant sections in this book. It is my fervent wish that all who read this book benefit from it.

This Book Will Bring You to a Mysterious Reality

- For parents raising children: Flip through the pages of this book and you will find clues on how to solve problems and will feel better.

- For elementary school children: Enjoy doing Quantum Speed-Reading with this book and seeing the imagery from it.

- For students doing examinations: When you are studying, keep a copy on your desk, and when you take exams, bring the book along as your new lucky charm.

- For the businessperson: Keep a copy in your briefcase and when your work seems to get stuck, just flip through these pages.

Today in Our Classes

Children currently attend our classes full of joy. During the writing of this book, new talents were uncovered and continue to evolve. I will take the opportunity to write about these discoveries at a later date. It is, of course, challenging to spread the word about this work by talking to one person at a time, so I would be very happy if this book succeeds in bringing our message to many readers.

In closing, I would like to give my heartfelt thanks for the editing of this book to Izumi Sakai, Naoko Mianishi, and Naoki Fujii. I am also very grateful to Terashita of the Kasai school, who has helped me from the inception of Quantum Speed-Reading. And without the cooperation of the following people, this book would not have been possible: Takahara, Jun Masayama, Maeda, and Toko Fukuyoshi (for her charming illustrations [in the original]). Finally, to all the children who have helped me all along in class, I would like to give my deepest thanks.

About the Author

Yumiko Tobitani is a leading teacher at the Shichida Child Academy (SCA), with previous experience at the foreign exchange department of the Tokyo Bank. After having managed a prep school, she joined the SCA in 1992. Based on her experience in the educational field, she has developed the Dot Program, the Right Brain Memorization and Sensory Training Program, Quantum Speed-Reading, and the Right-Brain Speed Calculation System, among other achievements. She is also involved in conducting seminars for adults in right-brain development. She currently heads the research and development branch of SCA and is a member of both the Human Science Association and the Subtle Energy Association of Japan. For more information please visit www.quantumspeed reading.com.

About Makoto Shichida

Makoto Shichida, who wrote the foreword and served as an advisor in the writing of this book, was born in Shimane Prefecture in Japan in 1929. He is a professor of education and a lecturer at the School of Education, Newport University (Japan Campus). Shichida is also the Chairman of the Shichida Educational Research Center and the principal of the Shichida Child Academy, which currently has over 400 schools operating in Japan. Schools are also spreading throughout Taiwan, Korea, and the United States. He was awarded a Special Medal of Recognition for Contributions to World Peace at the World Intellectual Property Registration Conference held by the Union Academique International (International Union of Academies). He also received the Sociocultural Service Award in 1997 and was awarded the Grand International Science Prize by the World Science and Culture Council. Shichida has written more than 50 books, including *The Science behind Intellect and Creativity* (Nippon Jitsugyo Publishing) and *The Right Brain Revolution* (Sogo Horei Publishing).

Hampton Roads Publishing Company

... for the evolving human spirit

HAMPTON ROADS PUBLISHING COMPANY publishes books on a variety of subjects, including metaphysics, spirituality, health, visionary fiction, and other related topics.

For a copy of our latest trade catalog, call toll-free, 800-766-8009, or send your name and address to:

HAMPTON ROADS PUBLISHING COMPANY, INC.
1125 STONEY RIDGE ROAD • CHARLOTTESVILLE, VA 22902
e-mail: hrpc@hrpub.com • www.hrpub.com